The end of the experiment?

MANCHESTER
1824

Manchester University Press

The *Manchester Capitalism* book series

General Editor

MICHAEL MORAN

Manchester Capitalism is a series of short books which reframe the big issues of economic renewal, financial reform and political mobilisation. The books do so by directly tackling such issues and the underlying conditions of the capitalist imagination in everything from university pedagogy to market bricolage. The underlying economic assumption is that a fundamental reframing of policy choices is necessary before we can reform our capitalism levered on the state, which is in turn levered on debt in all the high income countries. We write in the liberal collectivist tradition of the 1930s about new social techniques to ensure security in a resilient, responsible capitalism. But, we cannot share the faith of Berle or Macmillan in the benevolence and competence of central states, which in the present conjuncture are endlessly repeating experiments in competition and markets without confronting the limits of this framework.

The individual books in our series all combine 'follow the money' research with readable discussion of narrative alibis. This distinctive form of analysis was pioneered, in public interest reports about mundane activities like meat supply and railways, by the multi-disciplinary team of researchers working at the Centre for Research on Socio-Cultural Change (cresc.ac.uk) and now blogging at the Manchester Capitalism web site. Present day knowledges are combined with eclectic borrowing from free-thinking earlier critics of capitalism like Wright Mills and Braudel, who deserve better than the neglect of posterity. Our political assumption is that there is much distributed intelligence in our economy and society outside the metropolitan centres of elite decision making. We write to inform and empower that force which the nineteenth century recognised as agenda setting, provincial radicalism, and we promote devolved government with a social purpose for the twenty first century.

The end of the experiment?

From competition to the foundational economy

Andrew Bowman, Ismail Ertürk, Julie Froud,
Sukhdev Johal, John Law, Adam Leaver,
Michael Moran and Karel Williams

Manchester University Press

Published by Manchester University Press
Altrincham Street, Manchester M1 7JA, UK
www.manchesteruniversitypress.co.uk

British Library Cataloguing-in-Publication Data
A catalogue record for this book is available from the British Library

Library of Congress Cataloging-in-Publication Data applied for

ISBN 978 0 7190 9633 4   paperback

First published 2014

The publisher has no responsibility for the persistence or accuracy of URLs for any external or third-party internet websites referred to in this book, and does not guarantee that any content on such websites is, or will remain, accurate or appropriate.

Typeset by Servis Filmsetting Ltd, Stockport, Cheshire
Printed in Great Britain by Bell and Bain Ltd, Glasgow

Contents

List of exhibits

Acknowledgements

The team of authors, from the Centre for Research on Socio-Cultural Change (CRESC), aims to work outside disciplinary constraints and produce research that is conceptually minimalist, empirically resourceful and politically resonant. In writing this short book, and planning similar books in the *Manchester Capitalism* series, we have been imaginatively supported by Emma Brennan in her role as Editorial Director of Manchester University Press.

Our research and drafting on the three sector case studies was by Andrew Bowman as lead author; with Mike Upton and Daniel Tischer working as research assistants to produce first drafts of the dairy and banking cases respectively. The argument in the introductory and concluding chapters comes out of conversation between authors from different disciplinary traditions: political economy, business and management, science and technology studies and political science are all represented in the team.

Non-academics have played a key role in developing our thinking. Our work with Enfield Council in North London started a train of thought about local economic experiment; and our understanding of post-1979 policy was stimulated by Peter Folkman's insight that privatization was a new sale of the monopolies. The broadband case benefited from input from Walter Willcox and the other cases have had some input from practitioners.

Our greatest academic debts are to John Buchanan (University of Sydney) for helpful criticism of earlier drafts and to Ewald Engelen (University of Amsterdam) for insisting on the relevance of Braudel. We would also thank Marta de la Cuesta (UNED, Madrid), Valérie Revest and Véronique Dutraive (University of Lyon) and all the participants at a Manchester workshop on the foundational economy in January 2014.

The finished book is our experiment. It is the collective result of team effort and a process of production and revision by many different hands so that our individual contributions were always transformed by combination with the work of others. In this way, the team of authors helped by their circle of friends, tried to mobilise the intellectual resources to shift economic and political thinking towards some useful learning

List of abbreviations

AFAP	Alternative frameworks are possible
ARPU	Average revenue per user
ATOC	Association of Train Operating Companies
BBA	British Bankers' Association
BDUK	Broadband Delivery UK
BIS	(Department for) Business Innovation and Skills
BoE	Bank of England
BOGOF	Buy-one-get-one-free
CRESC	Centre for Research on Socio-Cultural Change
CSR	Corporate social responsibility
DCMS	Department for Culture, Media and Sport
DEFRA	Department for Environment, Food and Rural Affairs
DTI	Department for Trade and Industry
FCA	Financial Conduct Authority
FiiC	Free if in credit (bank account)
FLS	Funding for Lending Scheme
FSA	Financial Services Authority
FTTC	Fibre to the cabinet
FTTP	Fibre to the premises
GCA	Groceries Conduct Adjudicator
GDP	Gross domestic product
GPO	General Post Office
GSCOP	Groceries Supply Code of Practice
GVA	Gross value added
ICB	Independent Commission on Banking
ISP	Internet service provider
LLU	Local loop unbundling
Mbps	Megabit per second
MFI	Monetary Financial Institution
MMB	Milk Marketing Board
NAO	National Audit Office
NFC	Non-financial corporation

NFU	National Farmers Union
NGA	Next generation access
NGO	Non-governmental organisation
OECD	Organisation for Economic Co-operation and Development
OFT	Office of Fair Trading
ONS	Office for National Statistics
PCA	Personal current account
PCBS	Parliamentary Committee on Banking Standards
PFI	Private finance initiative
PLC	Public limited company
PPI	Payment protection insurance
PPP	Public-private partnership
PSBR	Public sector borrowing requirement
QE	Quantitative easing
RGU	Revenue generating unit
RoE	Return on equity
SME	Small and medium size enterprise
STS	Science and technology studies
TINA	There is no alternative
TINAF	There is no alternative framework
UKFI	UK Financial Investment
WLR	Wholesale line rental

Chapter 1

The 30 year experiment:
imaginary, history and cases

Britain's relative economic decline throughout the 20th century – the so-called 'British disease' – was a national embarrassment that only went away in the 1980s. This column presents new research showing that competition provided the cure... .The results of the 'Thatcher Experiment' in the 1980s make the case and paved the way for reversing relative economic decline. Competition was much strengthened by ongoing trade liberalisation, deregulation, and discontinuing 1970s' industrial policy... At the sectoral level competition and greater openness were correlated with improved productivity performance.
Nicholas Crafts writing on his research in the VoxEU blog (2011a).

When the gas and electricity businesses were privatised in the 1980s, the Conservative government promised a competitive market that would deliver a better deal for consumers, competitive prices and sustained investment. Over 25 years later, it is acutely clear that privatisation has failed to deliver on this promise. Gas and electricity prices are uncompetitive. Bills are rising year on year. The market has failed to unlock the investment the country needs ... A One Nation Labour Government will reset this market to ensure we deliver on the original promise of privatisation. We will create a genuinely competitive market that works for Britain's families and Britain's businesses.
Ed Miliband and Caroline Flint introducing a Labour Party green paper on energy (Labour Party 2013).

Introduction

Britain is a country in secular decline, gripped by an imaginary about competition and markets which sustains an obsessive-compulsive experiment. The imaginary fuses assumption and assertion as in the two opening quotations, so that the medicine must work and different treatments are inconceivable. Within that imaginary, increased competition after 1979 cured the British disease; remaining problems in the 2010s can be solved by *more* competition. This framing, how 'competition provided the cure', dominates. The leading British economic historian Nicholas Crafts cites gross domestic product (GDP) per capita and productivity figures which support his argument about British relative economic performance; and, equally, cites none of the figures on housing equity withdrawal or the return of trade deficit, that would raise questions about the sources and sustainability of UK growth. Within this imaginary, anomalies and disappointments are recognised only to be explained away as problems arising from incomplete implementation rather than defective treatment. This is the response of Ed Miliband when considering how gas and electricity privatisation has 'failed to deliver on its promise'. Labour's solution is to 'create a genuinely competitive market that works for Britain's families and Britain's businesses' (Labour Party 2013) which will finally deal with the problem of high prices and low investment.

A combative right wing economic historian and a struggling leader of the Labour Party are not representative figures of national economic thinking, but their imaginary is doxa for the political classes in Westminster and Whitehall. Elite responses have become an echo chamber reverberating with one simple message endlessly repeated regardless of circumstances. For example, in retail banking, where behavioural problems range from mis-selling of personal finance products to unwillingness to lend to small business, the only focus for reform in Westminster is greater competition. This has been at the centre of proposals from all the UK's post-crisis official enquiries into banking, and parliamentary debates now include a form of one-upmanship over who is most committed to securing the competitive ideal. On the launch of Labour's proposals to create new additional challenger banks from state-owned Lloyds and RBS, the shadow chief secretary to the Treasury Chris Leslie stated: 'We have got to give customers more choice. Fees and charges are too high. There is not enough of a sense of competition, a hunger among the banks to serve customers' (BBC 2014). The Conservative Party's retort was predictable: 'David Cameron's long-term economic plan is about fixing our banking system – by increasing competition on the High Street, ring-fencing retail from investment banking so that no bank is too big to fail, and increasing lending to business … There is already greater choice on the high street now than there was under Labour' (BBC 2014).

Within this imaginary, new events do not challenge but confirm what the political classes already know, despite evident contradictions. In banking, the desirability of competition is grounded in belief in free markets, yet after decades of light touch regulation the only way left to securing it is through arbitrary state intervention which splits-up companies formed through processes of competition and consolidation. In energy, a quarter century after privatisation began in 1990, there is confusion over whether the continued absence of the desired market is the fault of buyers or sellers. So it was when the electricity companies were slow to reconnect consumers after storms over Christmas 2013. Tim Yeo, Conservative chair of the energy select committee, immediately accused the energy companies of 'utter complacency absolutely typical of a monopoly' (Chazen 2014). Two months earlier, his party leader, David Cameron had chosen in a contradictory manner to pin some of the blame on consumers during a debate about high fuel prices, asserting: '[t]here is something everyone can do, which is look to switch their electricity or gas bill from one supplier to another' (Read 2013).

What we have here is an imaginary that frames the world. Like all imaginaries it is a framework that provides an account of what matters in the world and how the world works; so it also serves as a blueprint for performative experiments that will change the world. In using the term 'experiment' we are not invoking hypothesis testing, nor the Large Hadron Collider built to test the existence of particles such as the Higgs boson. Performative experiment on the economy is (or should be) more like the clinical trial of treatments where the aim is to establish the safety and efficacy of the drug or device. The standard clinical test procedures involve control groups and varying doses on a population of patients, often in various stages of disease. Under these conditions, as tests are scaled up from pilots to large populations, it quickly becomes quite complicated to determine whether the treatment works (or works better than alternatives). But the principle of clinical experiment is that it is the treatment that is at risk, and that unsafe or inefficacious drugs should be discarded.

It is within this frame that we understand the past 30 years of British economic history as an experiment (of course, without control groups and the other apparatus of natural science). The imaginary of competition became the dominant basis of economic policy in the early 1980s and licensed the 30 year Thatcher-Blair experiment in structural reform which continues under the 2010 coalition government. Over the whole of this period in Whitehall or Westminster, anyone who wanted a career in or around economic policy had to perform the experiment (whatever their private misgivings); central government policies as a whole were never monolithic but it became increasingly difficult to find other (non-economic) policy domains where competition and markets did not intrude. In public, the political classes can only choose between celebrating the experiment's success, or admitting to disappointments that require redoubled efforts to make the experiment work. They cannot admit that their drug does not work.

The imaginary creates a self-sealing world where non-competition is self-evidently bad; the solution is more competition to improve national macro-economic performance and deliver sectoral micro benefits. Within this frame, the end of the 30 year experiment is an outcome which is not yet within the realms of the thinkable and doable. However, this book is written in the hope and belief that the imaginary can be unsettled and the experiment can be called into question. To adapt Gramsci, this kind of interrogation requires optimism of the will and activism of the intellect. It requires destruction of a world that is taken-for-granted, as well as the reframing of policy choices. The aim is to do so in ways which do not rehearse old and displaced orthodoxies, but reflect what has changed in the past 30 years both in economy and polity, and the tools needed to reconceptualise this. Thus we shift the object of analysis from the supposedly self-evident disease to the imaginary behind the treatment and we argue that, by the 2010s, large sections of the British economy are not suffering from economic disease, but from a policy experiment which continues fundamentally uncriticised despite the perverse and unintended consequences of the treatment.

The aim of this introduction is threefold and reflects an approach that draws together a multi-author team. First, in the next section we draw on Science and Technology studies to argue against naïve metaphors of national disease, highlight the imaginary (or cosmology) that frames those metaphors, and draw out the implications of our preferred metaphor, experiment. After arguing the need for the analysis of specifics, the remainder of this chapter introduces these specifics through a description of national peculiarities and sectoral cases. Thus, the following section provides context in the form of a broader political history of the role of 30 year policy experiments in post-1945 Britain, and shows how competition came to be the cure for British decline. The final section then shifts into political and cultural economy and engages specifics differently as it explains how our three sectoral case studies – telecommunications, supermarkets and retail banking – reveal the limits of treatment by competition.

The extended case studies are crucial because they show how competition (as policy goal and corporate alibi) creates industries that do not serve the national welfare. In all three sectors, the business models of the major corporate players are extractive. This is because they aim to maximise profit and cash by limiting investment; and they improve margins by hitting on consumers and suppliers. Our argument is that case specifics reveal crucial lessons about, for example, the need to shift focus by attending to business models and their consequences for supply chains. When the perversity of economic outcomes has been demonstrated in three case studies in chapters two, three and four, our concluding chapter takes up the difficult task of reframing the problems so that we can think about an alternative and how we might create it.

The only way to displace one imaginary is with another; and the only thing to do about the single-minded commitment to a bad experiment (one that administers the same treatment regardless of consequences) is to propose alternatives, and we suggest decentralised experiments which make space for learning. Thus, our concluding chapter does not end with policy recommendations but with an argument for a broader alternative vision in two specific respects. First, after thirty years of failure in tradable goods, we argue that the British need to focus on another, more mundane and sheltered economy which we call 'the foundational economy' which delivers everyday goods and services. Not only is this an economy that is overlooked in the present policy climate, but the sectoral cases show how it is being damaged by point value corporate business models. Second, we argue that the crucial obstacles to policy reforms that might develop the foundational economy are not economic, but political. The over-centralised British state is also fundamentally a non-learning state because, while its political and managerial operators are able to recognise disappointments, they are unable or unwilling to attribute them to the imaginary, so that the same experiment gets repeated again and again despite the accumulation of perverse consequences.

In sum, this book is about the national failure of a 30 year experiment, the problems created and the opportunities that failure now presents. It is set in the context of a larger argument about how capitalism isn't working. On finance, we have, for example, published on how and why it is so difficult to reform banking (Engelen *et al.* 2011) and analysed the fragility of long chain finance demonstrated both in the 2008 crisis and again in the Eurozone and emerging markets crises. The three sectoral case studies make a different but related point about the destructive effects of purportedly 'pro-business' policies which encourage generically-conceived 'competitive' capitalist firms in the hope that they will bring jobs. The case studies show that a focus on short term competitive advantage favouring certain forms of business and their allied business models damages the foundational economy in a variety of ways. By implication, if we want benefits such as investment in infrastructure or strong supply chains, it will be necessary to limit the capacity of a certain form of capitalist firm to extract short term profit and redirect business models towards more social outcomes.

The conclusion argues that this can be done through a combination of a policy of social license and a new kind of governance for corporate business in the foundational economy. This kind of policy recommendation is not an atavistic leftism carried over from the 1960s and 1970s. In terms of lineage, our critical intervention aligns with the militant centrism of the liberal collectivists when they faced a capitalism that did not work in the 1930s. Harold Macmillan (1938) and J.M. Keynes (1936) argued that capitalism was incapable of creating coherent solutions to social problems that required physical investment, or were related to everyday necessities. The message of this book is that, in a different way, we now face similar problems.

Disease, imaginary and experiment

They used, when I first came in, to talk about us in terms of the British disease. Now, they talk about us and say 'Look Britain has got the cure. Come to Britain to see how Britain has done it'.
Margaret Thatcher in 1988, when becoming Britain's longest serving Prime Minister, cited in Gilmour (1992, p. 93).

Many economists borrow the language of disease when discussing the economy. But they do so without reflecting on how medicine recognises disease through framings, or on how those framings change over time and do not always lead to treatment which alleviates symptoms or save lives. When she opens the sick body what the doctor sees in one period in history is a disorder of the humours and bodily fluids, and in another, a cancerous tumour which requires the knife (and in the future, maybe a test to determine how quickly the cancer will spread). Mainstream economists who believe in their own scientificity find it difficult to accept that they have (and should question) a generic imaginary about the make-up and workings of the body economic; they also fail to recognise the difficulty of using abstract, general categories to guide action in a world of specifics.

Economic and medical conceptions of disease

Medical tropes, metaphors and analogies proliferate everywhere in modern economic discourse. As the opening quote from Crafts indicates, mainstream economists attacked the post-war settlement by borrowing and endorsing imagery about the 'British Disease' and its 'cure' which was used by Thatcher and others (Gilmour 1992, p. 93) as a political way of conceptualising British industrial decline relative to European peers, and of boosting pro-competition policies to reform industrial relations, privatise state monopolies and abandon under-performing conglomerates.

In 2014 the British economy is said to be in a state of 'recovery' from a prolonged post-2008 slump. An array of statistical indicators from consumer confidence surveys to automobile sales to debt/ GDP ratios become 'signs of life' and 'renewed vitality' in a patient that is 'regaining strength'. Confidence in this recovery is increased by the reduced threat of 'contagion' from the Eurozone. When in January 2013 Mervyn King, Governor of the Bank of England, first announced that there were 'good reasons to suppose that a gentle recovery is underway', he warned that government would have to undertake a series of structural reforms – particularly relating to banking – 'to restore the economy to full health' (King 2013). The IMF gave a more cautious prognosis in what the media calls its 'annual health-check' for the UK economy released in May 2013; but one year later in 2014 was much more optimistic about the prospect of a 'strong and sustainable recovery' (IMF 2013).

Behind the political spin, media commentary and expert interventions, a certain conceptualisation of what might be called 'the body economic' has become common sense. When we talk about 'the economy', it is taken for granted that we are talking about a singular entity, with well-defined mechanical relationships between different moving parts connected by metaphorical pipes, cogs and levers: interest rates go down, bank lending goes up; taxes go down, investment and employment go up. The dispute is then both about whether minor changes (income tax at 50p, not 45p) will have significant results, and about the effects of major policy changes such as quantitative easing where there is no agreed understanding of the mechanisms involved. Economic health is always a two-dimensional affair: for all concerned, GDP is the privileged measure, growth in aggregate output is the goal and decline in output is to be avoided. The body economic faces external threats to health (growth), but sickness ultimately resides in internal imbalances and imperfect relations between key constituent parts.

'The economy' as a totality of production, consumption and distribution activities is an invention of recent date. Indeed, it was only created in the mid-20th century. The object now described by economists was produced and reified by them through practises of measurement and management – in particular the creation of national accounts. 'Economy' lost its previous meaning as a type of process embedded within other forms of human activity, and became a separate, external realm of exchange, rational calculation and predictable relationships amenable to mathematical analysis (Mitchell 1998, 2008). In a longer perspective, the body economic was the outcome of a process of scientisation of what would have previously been called political economy, beginning in the late 19th century with the import of techniques developed within the natural sciences – most famously by William Jevons – and reaching maturity after World War Two with the neoclassical synthesis of Paul Samuelson and others. This created modern macro-economics in which discrete national economies could be measured, modelled and compared. Comparability was predicated on commonality, and created the scope for universal policy prescriptions based on unshakable fundamental principles – as is witnessed, for example, when the IMF advocates near-identical treatment by 'structural reform' for the ailments of Greece, Ireland and Portugal in 2011 as it did for Zambia, Tanzania and Mozambique in the 1980s.

The evolution of the body economic also bears important though less recognised similarities with changing medical conceptions of the human body over the past three centuries. In the era of what Jewson (1976) calls 'bedside medicine', medical practitioners relied on the patronage of a small number of wealthy patients. A physician focused on the specificity of ailments, seeking 'to discover the particularistic requirements of his patient in order to satisfy them to the exclusion of his ubiquitous professional rivals... the successful medical innovator was one whose theories offered the patient a recognisable and authentic image of his complaint as he experienced it'. Therefore, 'the sick-man's subjective experience of his symptoms were the raw materials from which the pathological entities of medical theory were constructed' (Jewson 1976, pp. 232–3).

However, the sick man was to be displaced from medical knowledge in Western Europe over the course of the 19th century. Bedside medicine was supplanted first by hospital medicine developed in the Parisian hospital schools and subsequently by laboratory medicine practised by German scientists who, as with contemporary political economists such as Jevons, sought to transplant the techniques and methodologies of the natural sciences into their discipline. In hospital medicine, with access to numerous corpses for autopsy and with the status of patients (now drawn from the poor) weakened in relation to practitioners,

> *the special qualities of the individual case were swallowed up in vast sta-*
> *tistical surveys... the sick in general were perceived as a unitary medium*
> *within which diseases were manifested. The consultative relationship*
> *took the form of a processing exercise in which the ambiguity and indi-*
> *viduality of each case was systematically eliminated by the application of*
> *foreknown diagnostic procedures.*
> (Jewson 1976, p. 235).

Laboratory medicine in the German university system in the mid-19th century applied cell theory and experimental techniques to medical problems, and further advanced this move away from a person-orientated cosmology towards one oriented to objects.

What we have called 'imaginary' is termed 'cosmology' by Jewson. A cosmology for Jewson means the

> *conceptual structures which constitute the frame of reference within*
> *which all questions are posed and all answers are offered. Such intellec-*
> *tual gestalt provide those sets of axioms and assumptions which guide the*
> *interests, perceptions and cognitive processes of medical investigators...*
> *Hence, cosmologies are not only ways of seeing, but also ways of not*
> *seeing.*
> (Jewson 1976, p. 225).

In the body economic, we can see a scientised cosmology which is very similar to that of laboratory medicine. In particular, the functioning of that body becomes the result of immutable laws played out in the interactions of individual units constituting a whole, unified by predictable relations and outcomes. However there is one crucial difference. In the forms of experimentation which underpin the cosmology of the body economic, the behaviour of the units that make this up is *assumed*. It is assumed that this takes the form of a rational, representative agent (firm or consumer) whose actions will create equilibrium in functioning markets. This means that the locus of disease is always the same: it is a consequence of insufficient competition between agents. And this in turn means that the universal prescription of greater competition can be applied confidently to economic problems at the level of the individual worker, consumer, firm, sector, city, region or nation. In our three case studies, we therefore find that these very different sectors have all been treated by reformers as microcosms of the body economic. The consequence is that the same treatments can, and have been, applied again and again. There has been complete confidence in the underlying premises and certain ways of seeing, which are also ways of not seeing.

Caught on specifics

The difficulty is rather obvious. It is that 'free market' economics – in its academic, policy and market populist variants – offers an *a priori* general theory of capitalist calculation where treatment starts from an abstraction of variables and generalizable relations. The result is that experiments then attempt to recreate those generalizations in the actually-existing specificity of 'the economy' and its constitutive units. Here STS work on scientific generalisations becomes relevant. This shows that generalisations can travel to different contexts but only under certain conditions. This usually involves reconfiguring the destination place so that it looks like the point of departure; put crudely, generalisations only become applicable if the world is operated on to fit the theory. In the case of 'free market' economics the point of departure is a textbook abstraction which ignores sectoral specifics and the resulting differences between various parts of the economy (Quiggan 2010). But the story of the past 30 years of economic policy experiment has been one of trying to build this imaginary by altering different sectors of the body economic to fit it. Surgical attempts have included privatisations, de-regulation and restructurings to create the conditions for uninhibited competition in sectors as far apart as manufacturing, the utilities, the labour market, housing, healthcare, food supply and education. And the results show the limits of this kind of performative agenda. Markets can be created and imposed, but these procrustean interventions come as a huge cost in the form of unexpected consequences driven by undisclosed, collateral, realities abolished (or, more accurately, rendered inconceivable) by the act of abstraction.

If they read and reflected on chapter 9 of James Scott's (1999) book *Seeing Like a State*, mainstream economists would see that their attempts to create a market are bound to fail in the same way as centralised socialist plans. This is because knowledge that is thin and impoverished cannot conceivably manage a world that is dense and rich. Practically, structural reform to enforce competition and markets comes up against the obstacle of sector specifics; as Scott writes, 'a mechanical application of generic rules that ignores these particularities is an invitation to practical failure, social disillusionment, or most likely both'. This means markets and the actors within them never work quite as expected and unintended negative social consequences proliferate: as Ed Miliband observes in the quote that opens this chapter, energy privatization has not delivered the promised benefits because energy companies bamboozle customers with opaque pricing systems and will not build new power stations without massive state support.

Much of our team's research work over the past couple of years has been to detail these unintended negative consequences. So, for instance, in the railways we have shown how the train operators have carved out profitable niches within a loss-making system while passing operating losses and capital investment costs to the state which has picked up the tab by taking on more than £30 billion of accumulated debt from Network Rail (Bowman *et al.* 2013a). The three case studies in this book add further examples of negative consequences: BT's monopoly power in telecoms cannot be diminished without further reducing socially necessary new infrastructure investment; supermarkets maintain steady profit margins by attacking their supply chains (including the dairy industry); and banks defend their high return on equity through all adopting similar business models which lead to mis-selling.

So this has been the experiment, one that has imposed – and continues to impose – a particular and abstract version of competition and market. Perhaps experiments of this form were understandable at the beginning because there was the prospect that lessons could be learned from new approaches to deep problems. But the continuing litany of failure and adverse side-effects suggests that the experiment has gone on for too long because it does not put enough at risk. Specifically, because it does not put the treatment or its framing imaginary at risk, learning is limited.

It is useful here to distinguish between what goes wrong on the one hand from what is put at risk on the other. If everything is specific, then in some sense every time a practice recreates itself this is an experiment. Necessarily, then, in an unpredictable world, practices will go wrong; but it is also possible to reduce what is put at risk in an experiment. More radical versions of science and technology studies are critical of self-sealing versions of scientific experiment that try not to put anything profound at risk but prefer to re-validate themselves. Looked at in this way, good experiments put more at risk: they build on successes and recognise mistakes, they make space for other *kinds* of experiments when they start to fail; they accept the treatment is not working and that the imaginary is being challenged. The problem for the UK is that, after more than thirty years, central government is still running the same competition experiment and prescribing the same treatment. Moreover, it is still explaining perverse results by using the imaginary to insist that things are going wrong because the experiment has not been pushed far enough.

If we wish to break with this circle, we must engage with specifics. This is why we explore the political history of British national peculiarities in the next section and write the extended sectoral case studies which are introduced in the final section of this chapter. Our argument about the framing of British economic policy and the need for reframing also has broader implications. Attention to specificity is not the equivalent of a return to the economic equivalent of bedside medicine, with the sector as the patient. It is more about expanding the ways of seeing the economy, paying attention to the undisclosed, and creating new possibilities for political and economic intervention. We take up this task in the final chapter and will here explain how it grows out of the preceding argument.

Any conception of 'the economy' is also and inevitably about a framing – both descriptive and prescriptive – which tells a story about foreground and implies (and in some cases actively seeks to sell) a policy *a priori* surrounded by undisclosed and collateral realities. It is not possible to avoid imaginaries, but if the circumstances are right it is possible to change them. In the present context this tells us that it would be helpful to heed Braudel's (1981) great insight that, although we have learned to speak in the singular about 'the economy', in fact there are many 'economies.' This insight makes it possible to create a space for the *foundational economy* that we discuss in the final chapter. This is another and different economy made of sheltered activities producing everyday necessities which of course include telecoms, supermarkets, dairy producers and processors, and retail banks. But the insight is political too because the focus on the foundational highlights the need for new forms of governance and an explicit system of social licensing in the foundational economy so that corporates are directed towards maintaining or improving their social performance in relevant dimensions. In telecoms, the first target would be more investment; in supermarkets, a better deal for processors as well as producers; in retail banking, reform of bank charges so as to improve transparency and reduce the pressure for mis–selling.

Our argument in chapter five is that all this is invisible and unnecessary because central government has stopped learning in a fundamental sense as it promotes the imaginary about competition, blames imperfect execution and adds bolt-on auxiliaries such as industrial policy. Our political analysis is that we are living in a state of non-learning and the political corollary is more devolution which would allow decentralised experiment.

National decline and two 30 year experiments

England's marvellous progress is an event of the past, not... of current history. In all our industries you find a steady slowing down; it is Germany which is in for the 'marvellous progress' now. England made hers when and because she had command of the World's markets.
E.E. Williams, *Made in Germany*, (1896, p. 5).

Since the 1890s Britain has been a country in relative economic decline. The British economy has been a laboratory of experimentation for the past century, as the practice of economic management in the UK has been developed in response to war-time exigencies and peace-time economic failure in tradeable goods. If we narrow the focus to the post-1945 period, it is marked by two thirty-year policy experiments (the post-war settlement and the Thatcher-Blair experiment). As we observe below, both experiments produced disappointment but the point of difference is that the second one continues, not only because the political classes are over-committed to the experiment but because of the absence of an alternative framework.

The post-war settlement

By the end of the 19th century it was clear that the economic lead Britain had opened up in the industrial revolution over other nations had closed, and indeed that nations like Germany and the United States had surpassed the UK in key measures of economic performance. That realisation, publicly marked in 1896 by the publication of *Made in Germany*, sparked a debate about 'national efficiency' (Searle 1971), that continues to shape thinking about economic management. The first 'national efficiency' debate led to reforms – principally those implemented by the Liberal Governments after 1906 – which we now recognise as the first foundations of the social settlement eventually created out of World War Two: an increasingly elaborated social security net; an increasingly comprehensive system of publicly funded universal health care; a central government committed to the active management of (un)employment; a welfare state controlled to a large extent by the professionals (for instance in health care and education) who delivered the services (Perkin 2003); a 'mixed economy' in which control of utilities was increasingly centralised on nationally organised public corporations; and a system of politics in which political contestation and competition involved struggle for control of a metropolitan decision making machine which exercised increasingly tight central control over territorial administration.

In the period of the 'glorious thirty years' after the end of the Second World War, that settlement had some spectacular successes. In the economy it delivered the greatest rise in living standards experienced in recorded history. In the social sphere it delivered, in contrast to the experience of most other advanced capitalist democracies, remarkably economical services not obviously inferior to those of more generously endowed welfare states. Esping Andersen (1990) classified the UK as a 'residual' welfare state but this nevertheless allowed for a health care system, for instance, which produced outstanding health outcomes with lower levels of spending than most national comparators (Moran 1999). And in politics it maintained a 'unified' United Kingdom with stable Westminster majorities untroubled by the uncertainties of coalition government. The price of universal welfare entitlements and multiple redistributions was a social overhead cost that was not extravagant in relation to other European countries, but problematic given the uncompetitiveness of British manufacturing.

What the settlement could not deliver was comparative success in tradable goods, where the under-performance of British-owned giant firms was dramatized by recurrent payments crises and enforced depreciation of the pound. The problems which had concerned E.E. Williams returned with post-war recovery: by 1970 West Germany, with 20% of the European Community population, had 40% of its manufacturing output (Cutler *et al.* 1989, p. 11); these problems were later compounded when Japanese firms arrived in the first wave of Asian low wage competition. The post Second World War settlement was increasingly disrupted by the decline of the old industries of the industrial revolution such as shipbuilding and textiles; reinforced by the decline of the 'new' industries established in the inter-war years, like automobiles and consumer electricals. As the 1960s and 1970s wore on, bolt-on policy additions such as indicative planning and industrial reorganisation, or primitive corporatism (with prices and incomes policy), either failed to deliver solutions or just added new problems.

The onset of global economic crisis in the 1970s, signalling the end of the 'thirty glorious years', showed the UK to be one of the most fragile of advanced capitalist economies. Even before the invention of 'Thatcherism' the failures of economic policy were also destroying confidence in the wider post-war social settlement: the history of the minority Labour Governments of 1974–9 amounted to an agonising draining away of confidence in that settlement.

The post 1979 experiment

The election of the first Thatcher Government in 1979 is a convenient symbolic moment for the beginning of a new experiment (one that took the form of dismantling as much as construction) to try to cope with the historic problem of decline. But it is precisely that – a symbol, rather than the moment of revolutionary change. That first election and the full impact of the great economic crisis in 2009 neatly bookend a thirty year experimental period during which key features of the 'Thatcher Revolution' were continued, and indeed deepened, under New Labour after 1997. But if the beginning of the great experiment can be traced to a single date it is more probably 9 June 1983, when a landslide parliamentary victory over Labour emboldened the radical instincts of Thatcherite Conservatism.

After that, the outlines of the great experiment became increasingly clear. It had six features which partly grew out of anti-bureaucratic, pro-market criticism of the post war settlement articulated since the 1950s in Institute of Economic Affairs pamphlets and such like; while all the major policies were pro-competition in intent, outcomes were inevitably more complicated.

- First, it aimed to flexibilise labour markets so as to empower managers. That process involved a mix of direct measures (legislation) to restrict the power of organised labour; the use of auxiliaries to confront particularly entrenched groups of organised labour (Rupert Murdoch and the print unions, the coal board and the National Union of Mineworkers); the exposure of industries where labour was particularly well entrenched, such as steel, to intensified competition via measures such as privatisation.
- That linked to a second key feature: dismantling much of the command economy which had been central to the management of public utilities. In the 1980s and 1990s Britain's privatisation programme was more extensive than that of any other leading capitalist economy, and its heart lay in utility privatisation:

telecommunications, energy, water and transport. This was reinforced by a culture change in the private sector as shareholder value
increasingly exposed managers to new pressures and one way or
another did for the old manufacturing conglomerates like ICI and
GEC which had anchored the industrial sector; policy reinforced
this by encouraging inward investment by foreign multinationals.

- Utility privatisation (with regulation to simulate competition) was
the chief 'headline' measure of the new settlement, but arguably a
third feature was even more profound, if only because its intensity
was maintained in the era of New Labour. Perkin had identified
professional power as the heart of the settlement of the thirty
glorious years; now central government set about reining back
that power. It did this partly by establishing systems of external
surveillance and control over professionals who delivered services:
the range spanned health, education, environment and incarcera-
tion. These are the changes summarised in Power's classic study
of *The Audit Society* (1997). It also more fundamentally changed
the ecology of welfare state professionalism by an ambitious programme of marketising and outsourcing service delivery. That programme ranged from the full scale transfer of delivery institutions
to the private sector (prisons for instance) to the transformation (as
in health care) of delivery administration into a web of contracts.

- This last change showed that controlling professionals was also
closely linked to a fourth landmark feature of the new settlement:
the wholesale outsourcing of professional delivery. The period
of the thirty year experiment saw the rise of a distinctive state
configuration which can be dubbed 'the contract state.' Its most
obvious institutional manifestation was the rise of new corporate
giants, like Serco and Capita, which lived largely off contracts to
deliver 'public' services. The range of franchising, viewed from
the perspective of the old professional, 'command' welfare state,
is striking: it stretches from the franchises at the heart of the
privatised transport systems to the management of public sector
pension delivery. And it brought with it a new model of state corporate relations as opportunistic bargaining.

These four developments – reshaping the landscape of power in
labour markets, large scale privatisation in an era of shareholder
value, dismantling professional autonomy, and outsourcing via a new
breed of corporate giant – were essentially institutional. They were
accompanied by two more contextual changes, one in the substance
of policy and one in its political management.

At the heart of the crisis which created the new contract state was the collapse in competitiveness of the industries (old and new, heavy and light) which had lain at the heart of British-owned manufacturing. The agonies of the industrial policy of the Labour Governments of 1974–9 also discredited any kind of industrial intervention by direct control, financial incentive or state reorganisation which had been used in the 'thirty glorious years'. The backstop of distress nationalisation of failed private industries, like cars in the 1970s, meant that central government was taking responsibility for intractable problems in ways that were bound to discredit it; in the event, the legacy of nationalising losers was a folk wisdom that government could not pick winners.

- There was indeed a consistent set of policies for competitiveness through structural change from the very beginning of Mrs Thatcher's election to office. It involved the liquidation of what were perceived to be the failing industries of the old economy, like coal – there was an obvious connection with other aspects of policy, such as confronting the traditional centres of union militancy and power. In place of that old economy were set two centres of economic regeneration: the creation of a 'branch economy' of multinationals, typified by the reinvention of auto manufacturing as branch assembly by foreign firms; and the self-conscious shift from a manufacturing to a service-based economy, the most high profile example of which was the reinvention of London as a global centre for financial services in the wake of the 'big bang' of 1986. Both had mixed results because London finance brought boom and bust through the housing market and added huge costs of bailout at public expense; and branch assembly meant just that, when nearly half the value of components in cars were imported in the 2010s.
- The five features of the new social experiment identified here, though they sometimes produced contradictory outcomes, can nevertheless be pictured as forming an intellectually coherent strategy. But there was a final feature essential to the whole enterprise which produced wildly contradictory outcomes. Privatisation in the economy and the creation of a vocabulary of marketization in public service delivery could be construed as part of a quintessentially Hayekian project: the 'depoliticisation' of social domains which in the former settlement had been viewed as the appropriate subject of political debate and intervention. But the new settlement was now marked by an unintended effect: increasing political micromanagement

from the metropolitan centre. The sources of this were twofold: dismantling professional autonomy (in education and health, for instance) exposed what hitherto had been a domain of professional control to intervention by democratically elected politicians, to the point where ministers were forming views about, for instance, the very details of teaching in classrooms; and the new contractualism of outsourcing provided little political cover for ministers when the delivery of contracted services failed, and forced intervention in the most minute details of service delivery.

An experiment in crisis

The result of all this dismantling and restructuring was more like work in progress than a new settlement; but that work in progress was in crisis even before the great financial crisis of 2007–9 because of four deficits: a competitiveness deficit; an accountability deficit; a competence deficit; and a social sustainability deficit.

- *Competitiveness deficit.* The international *competitiveness* problems of the economy were addressed by ceding corporate ownership and control to foreign enterprises which, by the mid-2000s, accounted for 40% of manufacturing output and most of the directly exporting factories; in parallel, the City of London was transformed into a booming offshore financial centre where hardly any of the main players were British. Thatcherism was a kind of wager that multinationals would be attracted to invest and expand by a flexibilised labour market. But, real manufacturing output in the 2010s was no higher than in the 1970s; and a 5% current account deficit in the third quarter of 2013 indicated that foreign firms (with an appetite for imported components) were just like their British owned precursors in that they were not generating the exports to cover the British propensity to import manufactures. The economy as a whole was reduced to occupying a subordinate position in the global division of labour.
- *Accountability deficit.* The fundamental *constitutional* impulse behind the post 1979 settlement had been the conviction that the old world of public ownership and command and control hierarchies was opaque and unaccountable. But the new world itself created new problems of accountability: a complex array of franchises, especially in utilities delivery, the terms of which were often almost immune to transparency; a lack of clarity concerning lines of accountability between elected politicians and the opera-

tors of franchises; a world of financial accounting that seemed as much designed to obfuscate as to illuminate; a corporate elite, especially in the City of London, whose behaviour (revealed in the aftermath of the great crisis) displayed an arrogant disregard of the constraints obeyed by normal citizens.

- *Competence deficit.* Apologists for the post-1979 reforms accused the post-1945 settlement of incompetence: state-owned, command and control systems could not summon up the appropriate level of institutional intelligence, and market-shaped institutions would be better at doing the job. Yet the new order brought no let-up in the stream of policy blunders around outsourcing and contracting: various forms of public private partnership promised risk transfer but created profit opportunities for the private sector with the state backstopping liabilities (NAO 2011; House of Commons Public Accounts Committee 2011). This raised questions about the role of an increasingly politicised civil service where advisers called the shots and civil servants increasingly lacked sectoral expertise. Furthermore, an exaggerated burden of expectation was placed on regulation which was manifestly ineffectual in the utilities, and utterly disastrous in finance where it inflicted huge damage on the economy and cost on the taxpayer. Incompetence seemed engrained in the new social order.

- *Social and economic sustainability deficit.* Moreover, as later chapters of this book show, that new order has increasingly revealed a social and economic sustainability deficit of the kind that concerned 1930s liberal collectivists when Harold Macmillan wrote that 'economic and social organisation' cannot 'satisfy the moderate needs of men for material welfare and security' (1938, p. 375). The most obvious example of social and economic problems lies in the provision of public goods. The post-1945 settlement did provide a stream of public goods; it also managed the social overhead cost by rationing health care and much else, while it cross-subsidised in all kinds of ways to create national systems of welfare. But the web of franchises and privatised markets that succeeded this settlement has been unable to match this. As we argue in the telecoms case in Chapter 2, the maximisation of shareholder 'point value' inhibits investment in infrastructure. The old command-and-control healthcare system was remarkably cost-effective by outcome measures; the transformation of the health system has been accompanied by an almost constant cost crisis. Meanwhile, the spread of low wages increases the demand for housing benefit and other forms of welfare.

Sectoral cases: telecoms/broadband, supermarkets/dairy and retail banking

The central chapters of this book present three extended sectoral case studies of telecoms and broadband, supermarkets and dairy, and retail banking. We would not attempt any kind of formal justification of the cases as empirically representative or theoretically significant. They are chosen for two reasons. First, the cases represent the next exploratory step for a research team which has become increasingly interested in the specifics and heterogeneity of the mundane activities in the foundational economy. Second, the cases have been chosen because they powerfully illustrate the limits of a generic competition and markets approach; it also gives us an opportunity to reframe the analysis using different categories like confusion marketing and business model. This section of the introduction therefore has a double aim: it explains the limits of the standard analysis and presents the findings from an alternative frame. Beyond this, we recognise that many readers will find the cases to be challenging because they are densely empirical, closely argued and necessarily engage with the financial aspects of business models. This section, therefore, also serves as an introduction to the arguments which should make the cases more accessible.

Telecoms is a classic utility where the state monopoly was privatised in 1984 so that we now have 30 years of experience of privatisation with attempts to introduce or simulate competition through enforcing price reductions and encouraging competitors, and most recently by opening up the telephone exchanges. Supermarkets and dairy or retail banking are both sectors where competition takes the same form of oligopoly in a retail market dominated by giant chains, which interestingly has apparently different results in the two sectors: supermarkets claim the credit for serving the customer in exemplary ways while retail banks have been repeatedly criticised for poor service and mis-selling amidst allegations that they lend too little in business loans to small and medium sized enterprises (SMEs).

- In the foreground in the telecoms sector is BT, a giant public limited company (PLC) with turnover of £18 billion and pre-tax profits of £2 billion. After privatisation, BT inherited the state's monopoly telephone network which has since been opened up to competition in fixed line and broadband. What happened after BT was privatised is an interesting story because this is a fast-moving sector where technologies change and investment has been required with the growth of mobile telephony and broadband. However, there was also enough revenue from telecoms users to meet stakeholder claims. These circumstances are different from those in another privatised sector, railways, where our earlier work has shown there has never been enough money in the fare box to meet all the claims, including investment. In rail, a privatised structure created opportunities for private players to create profitable niches in a loss-making industry and pass investment costs to the state (Bowman *et al.* 2013a).

- Supermarkets and dairy feature retail competition between four or five giant public companies accounting for 80% or more of the market. The big four in supermarkets (Tesco, Sainsbury, Morrisons and Asda) are all PLCs; and the big 5 high street bank chains (Barclays, HSBC, Lloyds, RBS and Santander) were likewise all PLCs until the distress nationalisation of RBS and Lloyds. Their activities are important in themselves when, for example, the big four supermarkets directly employ nearly 800,000, and the bank monopoly on payments ensures that nearly 95% of British adults have a current account. We had already worked on the relation between supermarkets and meat suppliers (Bowman *et al.* 2012a), so dairy was an opportunity to extend that analysis. We had also previously worked on banking (CRESC 2009) but had concentrated on investment banking and financial markets, so retail banking was a new object.

In all three sectors, the case studies are historically informed, empirically resourceful and conceptually minimalist. The authors have no commitment to any particular school of political economy; they do not start from a position on the sources of value, the conditions of stable growth or the role of institutions. The cases present the results of exploratory analysis of how things work out (and do so rather differently from what we would expect from competition and markets predictions). We demonstrate this with our 'method' of observing the discrepancies between two domains. This involves following the money around the sector and then relating numbers and narrative. In this way we find a discrepancy between financial results and the (often non-financial) promises and achievements declaimed by the advocates of privatisation and defenders of competition (as well as by self-serving trade narratives) which have together created an imaginary about the competitive process and its results. All is not as it is claimed to be in this imaginary and we find a pattern to the discrepancy because, in each of the three cases, the flow of money around the sector explains social disappointments like the slow roll

out of new technology in broadband, farmers and processors struggling in the dairy sector, and mis-sold customers in retail banking.
Each case therefore tells a different story about how competition
produces disappointment.

- In telecoms the disappointment is about underinvestment.
  Privatisation was sold with the promise that it would free-up
  investment in new technology which had been rationed by the
  Treasury when the network was under public ownership. At the
  end of the 1980s, private investment by BT led to installation
  of labour-saving System X exchanges (a technology developed
  under public ownership). Thirty years later, BT is now delivering
  a network of high-speed broadband through fibre optic cable;
  but this is technically compromised because BT runs fibre to the
  cabinet (not to the premises) and has to be paid by the state to offer
  high speed connectivity to firms and households in areas of low
  population density. BT is investment-averse because capital investment in a fibre network competes with dividend distribution and
  share buybacks; investment in fibre also competes with spending
  on sporting rights which increase BT's market share in subscrip-
  tion TV. BT now competes against other telecoms service providers, including Virgin which has its own cable network. However,
  BT's competitors will not invest in network extension because
  they prefer to make profit from urban customers. The sector thus
  behaves much like the private providers of telephone services
  before 1914, which created the demand for nationalisation.
- In supermarkets and retail banking the disappointment is about
  injured stakeholders, the supplier in supermarkets and the customer in banking. In supermarkets there is a supply chain
  involving dairy farmers and processors. Dairy farmers have long
  complained about oppressive conduct by the supermarkets but
  our financial analysis highlights the plight of the processors (especially in liquid milk) which have become the squeezed middle
  of the chain. The processors' revenue share of a litre of milk fell
  from 35% to 19% over the decade after 2001. Processors are
  silent victims because they do not have the cultural capital of
  the farmers and are inhibited from speaking out by their direct
  dependence on supermarket orders. In banks, it is the customers that are squeezed. In the absence of a supply chain, the retail
  banks have hit on customers and use their branches for pressure
  selling of fee-earning products. The result has been repeated scandals about mis-selling to ignorant victims, most recently through

staff incentives to sell highly profitable protection products like PPI and interest rate swaps. The drivers in both sectors are financial because giant PLCs compete in two dimensions: first, in the product market to win customers; and second in capital market to earn the margins required by the stock market. And in both cases, margins for the shareholder are maintained at the expense of another stakeholder, so the stories of competition in retail banking and supermarkets/dairy are less different than they seem.

In the imaginary of those who recommend competition, the latter is a generically beneficial process which curbs profit margins and delivers lower prices. But the cases show that, while competition between PLCs plays out in different ways, the outcomes are socially dysfunctional in all three sectors where the shareholder and stock market returns are always privileged. In supermarkets and retail banking, higher returns are achieved by hitting on another stakeholder; in telecoms, the pressure to secure high returns stands in the way of socially-useful investment in high-speed broadband. As for profit margins, if we look at the benchmark of return on equity, margins are remarkably resilient and price competition does not seem to be working as it should in the imaginary.

In supermarkets and banking we see margins maintained semi-permanently despite competition. In supermarkets, there is an endless struggle to gain like-for-like sales and the balance of advantage shifts from one chain to another, and yet the stock market still expects 10% return on equity performance from a successful supermarket chain. Pressure from below by hard discounters may reduce margins in the next phase but the remarkable point is that this kind of target has stood in retail for twenty years. In retail banking, since Lloyds set a return on earnings target of 18% in the mid-1980s, the sector as a whole has delivered 15%, and nothing has changed since 2008 because Barclays is still aiming for those kinds of returns. In telecoms, the picture is more mixed because BT's overall corporate margins hold up but in some segments, like broadband, competition has depressed margins on sales for a challenger like TalkTalk. In this case, it is clear that the results include both lower prices and reduced basic investment in network extension. Thus, TalkTalk can earn a return on capital of 15% but only by avoiding large scale investment and focusing on customers in more densely populated areas.

This leaves an interesting puzzle: how and why are the major corporates able to maintain margins when they ostentatiously compete amongst themselves? In the supermarkets, for example, the great expansion of the chains dates from the abolition of resale price maintenance in 1964; and, in more recent times, a succession of competition inquiries has demonstrated that there is no covert collusion between chains to fix prices. From the three cases, we conclude that the results which were once produced by price fixing and collusion are now being generated by other means: first, by the devices of confusion marketing which are used in the retail market by all three sectors; and second, by mechanisms of stereotyped competition in which all the major players adopt similar business models as in supermarkets or banking.

Confusion marketing is an important device which protects margins against competitive erosion. The core of the practice is redesign of products and marketing techniques so that consumer comparisons of value for money become very difficult; this is often backed by incentivising staff to push products with scripts that forestall objections and aim for nearly instant decisions. In telecoms, the standard practice is 'bundling' which sells phone, internet and TV as packages with the aim of squeezing more revenue from the customer and hiding the expensive item in an attractive package. In banking, since the mid-1980s banks have offered free current accounts which give away the core retail product and then recover the cost by opaque charges for unauthorised overdrafts, low interest on credit balances and the cross-selling of mortgages and other fee earning products. In supermarkets, instead of sustainably low prices across the basket, chains like Tesco and Asda make time-limited, constantly changing special offers on footfall drivers such as milk and meat.

Confusion marketing produces vexation for consumers in broadband, serious harm to consumers of financial services and the displacement of the burden of waste onto the consumer of groceries. In supermarkets, consumers are buying products that they do not need, so that that they throw away around one quarter of perishable purchases. Some blame the consumer, and argue that if only consumers behaved more rationally all would be well. This kind of position is implicit in reports on banking reform which lament the inertia of bank customers when only 3% of bank customers switch current accounts each year. This position is naïve in a sector like banking where confusion marketing has been applied to undermine the consumer's ability to compare price and quality: why switch if you cannot work out which account is cheaper? Furthermore, where large scale switching does take place it gets incorporated into the confusion marketing and adds costs which are passed on to the consumer: in broadband, more than 20% of consumers switch each year and companies compete by opening call centres to make special offers and giving away routers, set top boxes and such like.

At a more fundamental level, the underlying mechanism which maintains profit margins is what we call *stereotyped competition* as in banking or supermarkets. This results when the major firms within a sector adopt similar business models that respond to supply chain specificities and exploit local power relations to obtain returns by squeezing the same class of stakeholder, as well as by avoiding direct price competition. As we have argued elsewhere (Froud *et al.* 2009), business models are defined by the two requirements of financial viability and stakeholder credibility, which even not-for-profit organisations like the BBC must meet. Stock market pressure in PLCs then inflects these general requirements in a particular way towards *point value*. This has two features. First, value is not considered as a stream of benefits over *time* and instead becomes what can be condensed and extracted at a point here and now; hence the preoccupation with current earnings and share price, because every shareholder is assumed to have ownership motivations much like those of a private equity firm at the point when it is near to selling out. Second, value is not considered from a *chain* point of view, and the issue is to maximise value at the point of transaction, privileging the financial benefits of the shareholder/stakeholder; profits are levered on suppliers and customers, with disregard for the social interest in a network of national production and for the longer term economic sustainability of quality forms of production.

Supermarkets or retail banks are perfect examples because, in each sector, a handful of major chains are all levered on the same stakeholder (either suppliers or customers) and all use confusion marketing to avoid direct price competition. The interesting point is that so much of this is undisclosed and not in the mainstream field of the visible. Partly, this is because of rhetorical confusions, where the enrichment of owners (howsoever caused) is lauded as 'wealth creation' and where profit is supposed not to matter as long as markets are competitive because consumers will *a priori* benefit from lower prices and reduced margins. If high returns persist, the mainstream explanation for high returns is barriers to entry; as in all those reports on banking reform which recommend new entrants, or so-called challengers, to solve the problems of the industry. In our view, the sectoral evidence suggests that this is most unlikely if new entrants adopt the same business model as the incumbents. The three cases imply that what we need is, not more competition in its present stereotyped form, but differentiation of business models around objectives concerned with social and economic sustainability over the longer term; as we argue in the conclusion to this book, this would require a new system of governance with social licenses dependent on meeting specified objectives.

Instead of social licenses for definite objectives, since 1979 we have had a generation of misplaced effort by successive competition authorities and industry-specific regulators whose mission is to realise the imaginary. After change has been politically sponsored by the executive branch of government, the technicalities are delegated to quasi-public sector regulators such as Ofcom in telecoms or competition authorities like the Office of Fair Trading. These agencies structure the rules and composition of the respective sectors in a manner which strives to realise the imaginary. This imaginary was central to the British style of regulation invented by English academic figures such as Stephen Littlechild, who devised the RPI minus x price cap formula, or Michael Beesley, who recommended opening up BT's network for use by other operators. The aim was to simulate or create competition and the main measure of success was prices and consumer survey evidence. More broadly, incoherent attempts to create competition have produced uneven results. In telecoms, after initial failure to create a credible competitor company to BT, Ofcom's task has been to force the monopoly to share its assets with other companies and so allow them to compete on a level playing field. In the case of the supermarkets, competition authorities have curbed further concentration, enforced some guidelines on contractual relations, and abolished the Milk Marketing Board in the 1990s while restricting the size of farmer co-ops. In banking, after a decade-long failure to increase competition, the central state is finally forcing the divestment of some Lloyds-TSB and RBS branches in the name of customer choice.

This last point about regulation and intervention to realise the imaginary has implications for whom we hold responsible for the different messes in all three sectors. Should we blame the company manager, the shareholder or the corporation as organisation? In our view, the answer is none of the above because the sectoral modifications and their inevitable failure are the responsibility of politicians and regulators. Our three case sectors are ostensibly controlled by private owners and so outcomes in each sector are commonly attributed to the work of corporates and market forces which have replaced earlier state planning. In fact this is highly misleading. Each sector is the creation of a particular form of centralised state planning aiming to turn the market imaginary blueprint into a reality.

This is political *planning* of markets because, as Karl Polanyi (1944) observed, the market has to be *planned* into existence. The problem is then that the planner's imaginary stays the same as disappointments accumulate: the solution is always more competition, new entrants, more informed consumers, and the sanction is a dressing down by a Parliamentary Select Committee.

The three sector cases also help change our understanding of the processes and outcomes which in the past decade have been labelled as financialization. There have been many definitions of financialization but some of the earliest, radical definitions of financialization pressed the idea that more profits and increased distribution ratios came at a cost in terms of less employment and investment. In Lazonick and O'Sulllivan's (2000) argument, financialization was defined as a process of 'downsize and distribute' which incidentally reduced investment and the firm's ability to innovate technically. In our later work (Ertürk *et al.* 2008) we added complication by emphasising that the process of financialization had a variable conjunctural logic; and we might now add considerable variation in sectoral logic. But maybe it is time to return to the idea of financialization as a burden because our three cases suggest that point value business models in major companies limit our ability to achieve nationally important social objectives.

The logic of inhibition works differently in network and chain sectors. In a network activity like telecoms, extension and future-proofing is compromised because both have an investment cost; while in supermarkets and banks, the branches are run according to management accounting calculations of the profitability of individual establishments, with no consideration for vertical consequences along the chain. Point value in utility networks removes the element of cross-subsidy central to the earlier construction of national networks through devices such as fixed price connection of rural households and businesses; point value also subordinates technical judgement to financial exigency which may discourage more radical and durable (though expensive) technological shifts. Point value applied to branches in banks or supermarkets imposes a horizontal logic with closure of branches that do not contribute; and no regard for chain sustainability because vertical disintegration and outsourcing normalises adversarial trader mentalities.

Business power without responsibility is a problem in all three sectors, but managers and companies should not be blamed for irresponsible models. In a sector such as supermarkets there are the beginnings of an alternative paradigm which meets the social and chain objectives of secure supply and more balanced profitability: Tesco's aligned milk pools and, even more clearly, Morrisons' vertical integration of meat processing, represent another way. From conversations with corporate managers and consultants we know that many consider corporate social responsibility meaningless unless the corporate business model is challenged and changed; and some would do things differently if they could build new kinds of organisational capabilities internally and were externally protected from shareholders.

The problem is not that companies are bad but that this version of capitalism isn't working: in the three sector cases, corporate business is about point value and passing risk, while avoiding social responsibility and the obligation to provide reasonable quality, sustainable, everyday economic services at accessible prices. The need is for something more than competition and markets with bolt-ons like industrial policy to deal with market failure in the commercialisation of early stage innovation. It requires a fundamental reframing of our problems. This is what we are attempting through concepts such as the foundational economy and the non-learning state; and their corollary is a new practice of intervention through licensing for social objectives.

Chapter 2

Telecoms and broadband: under-investment and confusion marketing

Overview

In mainstream UK politics, utility privatization is generally represented as one of Mrs Thatcher's great policy successes which symbolically separates us from the bad old days of the 1970s. Telecoms privatisation is singled out as a best case because, thanks to regulatory intervention, the sector has apparently delivered private investment and lower prices in a way that other privatisations have not. Our case analysis of broadband challenges all this. Thirty years after privatization, the sector is still dominated by BT, whose business model is about turning legacy infrastructure into distributable cash for shareholders; while BT's competitors are all, for one reason or another, equally investment averse. Hence the private sector is not building a future-proof high speed broadband network with fibre to the premises across the UK. Confusion marketing is used by all players to push product bundles of fixed line broadband; while BT is spending funds that could be applied to network extension on buying sports rights so as to increase its pay TV market share. Far from curbing such behaviours, regulatory intervention has produced perverse and unintended secondary consequences. The opening of BT's exchange network to competitors since 2006, has allowed BT to create a new, profitable Openreach division from the rents it charges competitors. In the telecoms sector, as in other utilities, regulators face an insoluble dilemma: if prices are forced down so that margins are reduced, then private investment will not be forthcoming. And so the regulatory agency becomes the promoter of Braudelian monopoly as the corporate players in telecoms must be allowed their margins and then, when network investment disappoints, they must be induced to invest with further incentives which are extravagant in the case of BT and rural broadband.

It is not for government to usurp the role of the market, to impose particular technological options, or to dictate the timing of their introduction. The government has no plans to require the creation of a national broadband network based on fibre optic cables. The choice of technology used, and the rate and extent of the introduction of new technology, such as optical fibre, is a matter for commercial judgement...

White Paper on Information Technology (DTI 1988).

... while the scale of the challenge involved in promoting NGA roll-outs is broadly acknowledged, the difficulty of persuading equity investors to approve such upgrades is still being significantly underestimated. The views of equity investors are crucial because without their buy-in, NGA builds become highly problematic. Equity provides around three-fifths of the capital made use of in European telecoms companies, and there are widespread concerns that the remaining two-fifths accounted for by debt have already left the sector over-leveraged ... operators themselves may conclude they cannot justify fibre against other uses of their capital, especially share buybacks, which can provide 15% returns at substantially lower risk ...

Four Steps for Fibre: How to Secure Europe's Super-fast Broadband Future (Howard *et al.* 2012).

Introduction

The quotes above explain and illustrate current problems in providing nationwide access to high-speed internet in the privatised and liberalised British telecoms network. Successive governments and regulators have insisted that private companies should ultimately make the decisions about whether and how to improve the network. As the Conservative Government explained in 1988 this is a matter for 'commercial judgement', not government control. The problem is that the calculations of these corporate players are not about the social benefits of a universal network. Instead, they are about maximising returns from their own position within that network in a context where more investment in infrastructure reduces distribution to shareholders and competes with other, marketing-related, expenditures like buying sporting rights. The government's aspirations for 'next-generation access' (NGA) sets a technically modest target of 24-30Mbps (megabit per second) download speed for 95% of UK households by 2017, which is well short of anything that might be considered either genuinely 'superfast' by international standards, or future proof. Yet, productive investment in NGA is inhibited when investors and analysts remind public companies like BT and BSkyB that spending on share buy-backs can earn 15% at low risk and extending fibre optic is unlikely to yield more.

This seems paradoxical because the earlier history of privatised and liberalised telecoms was one of apparent success, paving the way for later privatisations of gas, water, electricity and rail. Beginning with Cable and Wireless in 1981 and ending with British Telecom in 1984, telecommunications was the first of the major monopoly utilities in the British economy to be privatised – and at the time the largest stock market flotation ever completed. Newly-privatised BT put investment into digital exchanges and met customer expectations of better service and lower prices. Politicians justified privatisation with promises which have been repeated with each successive utility privatisation in the decades since, most recently with the Royal Mail: the capital market would bring the funds for badly-needed investment and competitive pressures would deliver efficiency and prioritise customer satisfaction.

Pre-privatisation, there was a real problem about state restriction (or, more exactly, Treasury refusal) of public investment in crucial infrastructure upgrading in the 1970s. This was solved in the decade after 1984 when mechanical exchanges were replaced with all-digital System X exchanges, a project begun under public ownership but taken forward under private control and completed by the mid-1990s (BT 2014a). This improved the service quality and was profitable for BT shareholders. Those who retold this story did not note that digital exchanges were also a kind of investment special case because they had return on investment characteristics more favourable than most other utility investments, including fibre optic: re-equipping the telephone exchanges allowed BT to save maintenance labour over a period where the company shed more than 100,000 staff (Kwoka 1993; Foreman-Peck and Manning 1988).

The experiment with privatisation and liberalisation was widely imitated abroad but it had specifically national conditions. Westminster politicians (Conservative and New Labour) and their civil servants have regarded public ownership as a generically-inferior model that was part of a discredited post-war settlement; the default antidote has been privatisation and out-sourcing. The inflection of privatisation towards liberalisation with regulation by agencies was made by a small cadre of economists, including Michael Beesley, Stephen Littlechild and John Vickers, who remained centrally involved for two decades in debates around what to do with competition in private utilities. As Vickers and Yarrow (1988) argued, privatised utilities could be made safe if regulators promoted competition in (or for) the market, or simulated competition through regulatory devices like price caps.

Thus, British privatisation and liberalisation did not represent the triumph of Hayekian ideas about the market as an information system, it was more a wager that the privatised utilities could be taken out of the domain of politics so that the 'market' (with regulatory guidance) would limit corporate power. The struggle of academic knowledge against political interference and corporate power was always unequal; it predictably failed in different ways in various utilities where regulators and politicians had generic preferences and regulatory tools which engaged only imperfectly with the specific characteristics of different sectors. The result was an increasing, undeniable gap between privatisation promise and outcome. This gap took different forms according to sector circumstances but generally undermined the political credibility of the privatisation project among the electorate, to the extent that recent polling suggests a majority (including a majority of Conservative Party voters) would like to see rail and telecoms re-nationalised (YouGov 2013).

In the case of telecoms, old problems return after one generation, albeit with new causes. The privatised industry of the 2010s has problems about dissatisfied internet customers and incapacity to invest which curiously echoes the Post Office Telecom public utility industry of the 1970s. Consumers are frustrated about prices, service and the reliability of claims about download speeds, now caused by confusion marketing, not old style rationing. Confusion is driven by attempts to squeeze more revenue from customers and manage switching by bundling phone, internet, and TV together with arbitrary line rental charges and 'fair use' data limits. For example, Sky Sports customers get 'free' broadband, while BT broadband customers get 'free' sports, which complicates comparison through programmes like uSwitch. Broadband connections are sold with advertised 'headline' data-transmission speeds, which Ofcom and uSwitch have found to be seldom achieved (Ofcom undated a).

More fundamentally, there is again a problem about funding infrastructural renewal. Unlike many other developed and middle-income countries, the UK is not building a next-generation network taking fibre-optic cables to the premises of households and companies and thereby providing a network which is high speed, high capacity and future proof. Instead BT is running fibre to street cabinets with the final connection through old copper wires. This saves BT money but means lower and less reliable speeds (dependent on distance from an exchange) and, as experts argue, potentially providing only a stop-gap upgrade. The other problem is that the stop-gap upgrade is not being rolled out as a national network with infrastructure provision in low density rural areas cross-subsidised from the profits of operating in the high density urban areas. The green boxes which are the visible sign of the new fibre network are now ubiquitous on city streets but not in low-income rural communities because BT could only find a business case for a new network covering two-thirds of the UK's households in predominantly urban areas by 2014 (BT 2012).

As the opening quote from HSBC indicates, the obstacle is no longer public sector spending caps, but private sector investors who demand discipline in capital investment and often prefer to apply cash to other purposes, such as dividends or share buy-backs. Beyond this, the more fundamental problem is that the forms of competition imposed by the regulators of a liberalised system further inhibit investment. After a false-start with Mercury Communications in 1981, regulation did not create an effective challenger to BT in infrastructure, but it did open BT's network through Local Loop Unbundling (LLU) so that today over 100 different companies in the UK provide fixed broadband connections (Ofcom 2012b). However, BT's competitors are unable or unwilling to invest significantly in new network infrastructure because they are fighting for market share with aggressive pricing which both drives down prices on existing infrastructure and problematises investment in new infrastructure. As for BT, it collects rental charges from its legacy infrastructure, predominantly built under public ownership, albeit under tricky conditions as the regulator pushes prices down. The unintended consequences include resources allocated to sporting rights to retain customers and investment rationing which requires state subsidy: three decades after the state passed on responsibility for funding telecoms infrastructure to the private sector, BT has been allocated over £1bn of public money to construct a rural fibre-broadband monopoly.

History: from public utility to natural monopoly

Telecommunications can only be provided by means of cables or radio…
it would not be right to license a multiplicity of operators in one area to
install overhead wires or to dig up streets, nor would it be practicable

from a radio spectrum standpoint, at least for some time to come, to license more than two national public telecommunications networks.

Kenneth Baker, Minister for Information Technology, to a Parliamentary Committee in 1983, cited in DTI (1991, p. 81).

Kenneth Baker, a Conservative minister of the 1980s, was stating the obvious: there is a physical limit to competition in fixed cable networks. But the framing of telecoms services and how this network should be constructed and operated does change sharply. The history of the last hundred years shows how telecoms was first remade in the image of a public utility so that a universal national network could be constructed by cross subsidy; then, from the 1970s onwards, economists reimagined telecoms as a market requiring state intervention to create competition.

The sense of *deja vu* is immediate if we consider how and why the telephone network was originally taken into state ownership. While telegraph communications had been monopoly-controlled by the General Post Office (GPO) since 1869, early telephone networks were run by a multiplicity of private providers alongside the GPO. The result was an inadequate network with problems about interconnections, quality and coverage because private providers aimed for profit by serving urban areas and left the rest to the publicly-owned GPO (Foreman-Peck 1985, p. 222). The present problems with BT and Virgin Media's urban-centred fibre infrastructure are a reprise of pre-1912 problems which motivated intervention by a reluctant state.

In 1912, the solution was to create a public utility that prioritised universal coverage: the entire network (except in Hull and a few other municipalities) was put into public ownership via the GPO (BT undated). For the next seventy years, the means to universality was cross-subsidy to cover heavy losses on the provision of new phone lines, especially in rural areas. In the mid-1970s, for example, the average cost of a new telephone line to unserved premises was £400, but a flat connection fee of £40 was charged nationwide (Lamond 1978). The heavy costs of digging trenches, fitting poles, pipes and ducts to reach every corner of the UK was cross-subsidised by long-distance call charges and public subsidy. However, restrictions on the latter, and political pressure to keep the former low, hindered investment. Consumers complained about excessive charges and months spent waiting for a new line; liberal economists criticised cross-subsidy which distorted the pricing mechanism, and business leaders warned about the UK lagging behind international competitors such as Germany and the United States (Langdale 1982; Lamond 1978; Solomon 1986). The key challenge for Post Office Telecom in the 1970s was the replacement of obsolete Strowger mechanical switching systems in telephone exchanges with GEC's new all-digital System X (Pye 1978). Post Office Telecom, and its successor after the 1981 Telecommunications Act, British Telecom, had steadily increased net spending on fixed assets from £626m in 1972/3 to £1456m in 1981/2; at the same time it had gone from being loss making in the early 1970s to a self-financing organisation generating over £450m profit (Parker 2009, p. 242).

This was not enough because only two System X exchanges had been installed by the end of 1981 (Williams *et al.* 1981, p. 161). BT management told the Treasury that around £2bn would be needed that year and in several subsequent years to create the digital network. With higher customer charges politically toxic and other funding options (e.g. bond financing) closed off by the Treasury (Parker 2009, p. 247), this would mean a sharp rise in the company's external financing limit, initially of £450m, and a knock-on impact on the public sector borrowing requirement (PSBR). Reducing the PSBR was an unshakable Treasury priority, and they demanded that BT instead first seek dramatic internal cost reductions, particularly in wages. BT management decided these would be impossible to achieve and the result was an impasse over funding infrastructure which spurred the first monopoly utility privatisation. As the then Chancellor of the Exchequer put it, 'many of our problems in financing BT's investment programme would disappear to the extent that the Corporation's assets could be transferred to the private sector' (Parker 2009, p. 247).

After BT's float in late 1984 – netting the Treasury £3.9bn, the largest amount raised on the stock market in history at the time – the company pushed ahead with rapid introduction of System X exchanges and the trunk network was fully digital by 1990. This was widely construed as a vindication of privatisation but in reality had much more to do with the special case characteristics of the System X programme. Exchange renewal saved huge amounts of labour because mechanical exchanges were much more maintenance intensive: BT's workforce fell from 243,000 to 125,000 in the decade between 1988 and 1998 as the UK network became fully digitalised. From this it was possible to maintain capital investment and keep stakeholders happy as the remaining work force was well-paid, customers got cheaper calls and investors received dividends (plus a 50% appreciation in share prices in the 1990s bull market).

The political project of privatisation through ownership change overlapped with what might be called the economic project of market liberalisation. Before privatisation had reached the political agenda, liberalisation had intellectual impetus as the public utility was reimagined as an inefficient monopoly which would not deliver innovation and value for consumers without competition (Wheatley 1986). In this frame, the problem was what to do when it was not economically sensible to construct another copper wire network and mobile technology was in its infancy.

Under these conditions, liberalisation took two forms: first, there was an attempt to create a challenger to BT, a strategy which failed; and, second, there was the introduction of a regulator to simulate competition, a strategy which succeeded well enough to ensure a permanent role for economist-led regulation. The British Telecommunications Act of 1981 enabled private providers to supply equipment to customers, and gave government powers to license new telecoms operators to provide network services (BT undated). Mercury Communications, a subsidiary of the recently-privatised Cable and Wireless, was established as a secondary provider from 1983. Mercury introduced some blue phone boxes but never came close to establishing itself as a national-scale challenger to BT. Construction costs, the difficulties of interconnections with existing networks and cold feet from investors, meant BT remained dominant into the 1990s (Parker 2009, pp. 246–7).

More significant was the creation in 1984 of an independent regulator, Oftel, removing government from the telecoms market in a move designed to drive 'cultural change' in the industry towards winning market share via lowered prices (Solomon 1986). The new regulator had some immediate success in manufacturing market-like conditions and simulating competition. Real price reductions were mandated by Stephen Littlechild's price cap formula on a Retail Price Index minus (RPI-) basis designed to produce 'efficiency gains'; thanks to System X, prices did fall by over 20% in real terms by 1990 while BT maintained a pre-determined level of service quality (Carsberg 1986). On this basis of apparent success, the failure of Mercury's challenge was an opportunity to press the academic framing of the role for regulation of natural monopoly.

In a 1981 report for the DTI, Michael Beesley, a transport economist, had recommended opening up BT's network for resale and use by alternative operators at controlled prices (Parker 2009, p. 244). The primary aim was to make prices match marginal costs of provision, and thereby control rents from BT's infrastructure (rather than directly control BT prices, as the 1980s formula attempted). In the early 1990s, Beesley's problem definition and solution were adopted as the framework for regulating the modern privatised telecoms system. Policy makers argued that 'the [free market] distortion which needs corrective action is the overwhelming dominance of British Telecom' (DTI 1991, para. 7.11). However, it was accepted that BT would continue to have unassailable economies of scope and scale compared to new entrants so that direct competition was a futile objective. The government therefore introduced Beesley's system of 'equal access', in which multiple private telecoms retailers could compete by purchasing the ability to use the network from BT at regulated prices, and passing savings on to consumers (Pye *et al.* 1991), while BT retained a universal service obligation (Ofcom 2005a). As the 1991 White Paper put it,

> *The central aim of the government's communications policy is to ensure that consumers, both businesses and individuals – have the widest possible choice of high quality services at the most competitive price ... open and vigorous competition is the best way to achieve this.*
> (DTI 1991, para. 6.1-6.2).

This regulatory foregrounding of competition has since been applied to broadband. From 2001, Ofcom obliged BT to provide access at regulated, cost-based prices to the copper cables running from local exchanges to customer premises, the 'local loop' (Ofcom 1999). These reforms were subsequently adopted as law throughout the EU (European Parliament 2000). This allowed BT's retail competitors not only to buy wholesale network access but also insert their own hardware at exchanges and offer a differentiated product. However, by 2003 the newly-formed Ofcom was disappointed by the outcome of low LLU uptake and concerned about the fairness of wholesale pricing (House of Commons Trade and Industry Committee 2005). It lamented that commercial users of BT infrastructure had gone through 'twenty years of slow product development, inferior quality, poor transactional processes, and a general lack of transparency' (Ofcom 2004, p. 54). The regulator decided a more interventionist approach was required to stimulate greater choice and 'competition at the deepest level of infrastructure' (Ofcom 2005a). This resulted in the formation of BT Openreach in 2006, which BT cleaved out as a stand-alone subsidiary in order to stave-off regulatory threats of a full breakup. Openreach was required to provide full equivalence in terms of access costs and services to both BT's retail operation and its competitors. The difficulty was that Ofcom's remit included creating a favourable investment climate and this did not sit easily with measures designed to weaken the most likely source of investment, BT, by pressing down on the prices BT can charge on its wholesale products. The unintended consequence of such competition in telecoms has therefore been the difficulty of securing new infrastructure which serves wider social needs beyond the immediate economic interests of the market.

Today's challenge: fibre-optic and fast broadband

Competition has driven the success of the current generation of broadband services... the result has been greater choice, innovation, lower prices and high levels of broadband adoption.
(Ofcom 2010, para. 1.1).

The official account from the telecoms regulator is that broadband is a story of low prices and happy customers. The model eventually worked as intended by Ofcom: with BT obliged to provide wholesale access at controlled prices, some 100 different service providers entered the broadband business, including several major LLU operators, and prices have fallen (Ofcom 2012b). Between 2006 and 2012 the proportion of premises connected to an LLU exchange rose from just over 60% to more than 95%, while the average monthly cost of a residential fixed broadband connection fell from around £24 to £16.

However, by the late 2000s what consumers needed was new, high-speed broadband infrastructure. By 2012, basic copper broadband connections were available to over 98% of the population, and 80% of the population had a domestic internet connection (Ofcom 2013a, p. 259). But the legacy copper wire network only provides speeds of up to 20Mbps, depending on local network quality and average speeds are still well below this (Ofcom 2013e).[1] Extending what Ofcom calls 'Next Generation Access' (NGA) (or 'superfast' broadband), with a headline speed of over 24Mbps has become a government infrastructure priority (Department for Culture, Media and Sport 2013). This has not been straightforward, as Ofcom has been forced to juggle competing priorities between competition, low consumer prices and widespread access on the one hand, with profitability for the private sector operators ultimately responsible for choosing the technology and building the network. Ofcom's pivotal 2005 Strategic Review had included the principle to 'promote a favourable climate for efficient and timely investment and stimulate innovation.' This was done by attempting to provide 'a consistent and transparent regulatory approach', and 'estimating a reasonable rate of return' for BT (and any other providers, should they emerge) as a margin over its cost of capital which would incentivise it to build (Ofcom 2005c). BT eventually began building a new network in 2009 which it expected to become profitable, but coverage remained a problem. 'Superfast' connections have been available for several years from BT's fibre optic network (both to BT customers and wholesaled to other providers) and from Virgin Media's cable network. BT is investing to extend its fibre network where it can construct a business case, and claims it will be accessible to 66% of the UK at the end of this programme in mid-2014. Virgin is accessible to just under half of UK households in larger towns and cities, but it has no plans to significantly extend its network beyond this. To do so may risk Ofcom classifying them as a 'significant market power' like BT, and forcing them to share their network. As of June 2013, 73% of households had the option of NGA access via BT or Virgin, according to Ofcom (2013a, p. 320). The conundrum for policymakers has been covering the remainder of the population in a highly urbanised country where huge rural expanses remain uncovered.

A second problem is network quality. If the Boston Consulting Group is correct in estimating that the UK has, proportionally, the largest internet economy of any G20 nation, then it should be a frontrunner in every respect (BBC 2012a). This is not the case. While the UK fares well on broadband price and consumer uptake (Ofcom 2012a), the UK was ranked 12th in the OECD for *advertised* average download speeds in late 2012, and 22nd for median advertised speed (OECD 2012). A headline speed of 30Mbps is judged 'superfast' by the UK government, but is unambitious internationally. The European Commission is targeting 100% access to 30Mbps and 50% access to 100Mbps broadband by 2020 (European Commission undated). To achieve widespread access to speeds higher than 100Mbps and build in reliable spare capacity for future demand, the House of Lords Select Committee on Communications Committee (2012) suggested after an extensive enquiry that a fibre-to-the-premises (FTTP) network is almost certainly required – and this is what many other major economies are implementing. But while countries like Japan and Korea have already achieved FTTP penetration levels of around 50%, and Singapore requires all new homes to be fitted with an FTTH connection capable of 1Gbps, the UK does not enter Europe's top 20 FTTH rankings, with less than

200,000 connections (Broadband Commission 2013, p. 49; FTTH Council Europe 2013). BT rejected this option, which was estimated by government advisers to cost just under £30bn (House of Lords Select Committee on Communication 2012, p. 13), in favour of a cheaper fibre to the cabinet system (FTTC): fibre optic cables linking exchanges and street cabinets, with the final connection (typically around 300m, according to Ofcom) via copper wires. These connections are marketed as enabling download speeds of 'up to' 38Mbps or 'up to' 76Mbps and sold at a premium, but, as many dissatisfied consumers have found, actual speeds vary enormously according to the length and quality of the copper wires (Ofcom 2013a, p. 320).

Digital exclusion is now politically and economically unacceptable and so BT and Virgin's piecemeal provision has prompted state intervention: in 2010 the incoming coalition promised to create the 'best broadband in Europe by 2015', stating it would get 'superfast' broadband to 90% of the population and standard 2Mbps to everyone – targets which in 2013 were pushed back to 2017 at 95% superfast coverage (Department for Business, Innovation and Skills 2010; HM Treasury 2013b). Rather ironically given the reasons for privatisation, it is attempting to achieve this by providing public subsidy to make BT's rural investment profitable. The longer term issue is installing FTTP, or other systems which offer similar capacity. BT and small independent operators will provide on-demand FTTP, but at a cost ranging from several hundred to several thousands of pounds per connection to cover construction costs. If the 'to the cabinet' network is potentially only a stop-gap solution, where would the money for future upgrades come from?

Investment-averse private sector business models

> *Objectives like this [driving prices down through competition] may have had merit in the earlier stages of a given market's development, but our worry is that such behaviour seems to have become locked in, despite having long since lost its utility. For example, despite the increasingly saturated nature of the market for ADSL broadband services, in most countries there have been relatively few signs of an evolution in the nature of competition – with many players continuing to engage in ruthless discounting.*
> (Howard *et al.* 2012).

The answer to our question is that the funds for major investment in FTTP and in network extension to the rural areas are unlikely

	Revenue £m	Operating profit £m	Net profit £m	Capex £m	Dividends £m
2010	1,796	17	−3	107	267
2011	1,833	78	36	104	16
2012	1,712	147	140	107	59
2013	1,670	141	100	104	87

Exhibit 2.1 TalkTalk financial performance and investment, 2010–2013
(2013 prices)
Source: company annual report and accounts

to come from corporate actors. Their investment in infrastructure is doubly constrained by pressure from the stock market for higher returns and by pressure that results from the type of price competition imposed by regulators. This last point is made by the HSBC analysts in the quotation at the beginning of this chapter, who observe that in Britain and other countries, the corporate players in broadband are locked into modes of price competition that inhibit infrastructure investment. The business models of most major UK internet service providers (ISPs) are focused on winning market share through aggressive discounting, with minimal investment (achieved by renting access to existing infrastructure) so as to ensure good return on capital. BT is the incumbent with the infrastructure: it plays the same game from a different position, also fighting for consumer market share but supplementing its income with rents from other ISP providers paying to use its infrastructure.

TalkTalk exemplifies the former. With four million customers by mid-2013, it is the UK's fourth largest internet provider and runs the largest unbundled network covering 95% of homes through 2,724 exchanges (TalkTalk 2013). Despite rapid expansion, capital expenditure has not risen far above £100m (exhibit 2.1), always remaining below 10% of turnover with the company targeting just 6%. The company piggybacks on BT's infrastructure, achieving slimmer operating margins than BT Retail, but the low investment means TalkTalk achieves roughly the same return on capital employed as BT, at around 15%. Besides trying to lure customers with attractive pricing, TalkTalk has tried to boost profitability by enlisting regulatory assistance to control the wholesale price BT charges. To that end, TalkTalk's senior staff regularly criticise both BT for monopolistic behaviour and overcharging for network access, and Ofcom for allowing Openreach to achieve what it considers to be excessive returns (e.g. Ofcom 2013c; TalkTalk 2008; Wik Consult 2013). BT inevitably responds by noting TalkTalk has no intention to invest in infrastructure (see, for example, Armistead 2013).

BSkyB and Virgin are more substantial players which arrived in broadband from satellite and cable TV to offer product bundles that reduce customer switching. Just like TalkTalk, BSkyB, the UK's second largest broadband provider, relies on renting the BT network but unlike TalkTalk has the advantage of a large TV subscriber base. This gives it an advantage in winning and retaining market share, using TV charges to offer subscribers discounted broadband. BSkyB is coy about investment but that is unlikely to be running far ahead of TalkTalk's £100 million a year on installing its own equipment in BT exchanges.[2] This has nothing to do with transformational infrastructure and incidentally produced a pattern of uneven provision. As Ofcom explain, LLU involves sunk costs which deter many companies, and is 'subject to significant economies of scale and density' (Ofcom 2010). New entrants first clustered in exchanges serving densely populated areas leaving BT as the sole provider in less densely populated areas. In 2010, for example, there were 3,587 exchanges (covering 15% of the UK), which had only BT as the provider. Some 2,002 exchanges had two ISPs or more, with 1,171 exchanges offering four or more providers. Since 2010, the number of exchanges served only by BT has decreased to below 6% (Ofcom 2014), yet there are still significant rural areas lacking any alternatives to BT, or with very limited choice.

Virgin, the third largest ISP by customers, is a different proposition to BSkyB. As an urban cable TV operator, it uniquely has its own network infrastructure which can provide high-speed internet in urban areas. Virgin was born from the failure of the UK's cable TV franchises in the 1990s, and the coaxial fibres of the network provided a head-start in superfast broadband. Virgin claims a cumulative total of £13bn spent on its fibre network and annual depreciation charges for Virgin are now close to those of BT Openreach at over £900m (Virgin 2013).

In sum, new entrant ISPs may have lowered broadband prices but they have done little for infrastructure provision beyond replicating the pre-1912 problem of unevenness, because they cherry pick urban business and ignore unprofitable areas. The annual combined capital spend on broadband infrastructure by Virgin, TalkTalk and BSkyB nonetheless represents a considerable sum which is socially wasteful, either because it does not fundamentally improve the quality of the base infrastructure (LLU) or because it duplicates it (Virgin).

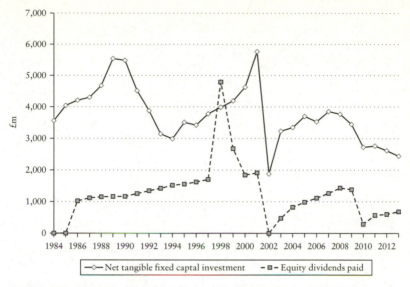

Exhibit 2.2 BT net tangible fixed investment and dividends, 1995–2013
             (2013 prices)

Source: company annual report and accounts

The responsibility for network transformation and extension falls
almost entirely to BT whose public narrative is about heroically shoul-
dering this burden by committing £2.5bn to 'superfast' infrastructure
between 2009 and 2015. The figure needs to be set in context. The
core of BT's business model is turning a legacy infrastructure into
distributable cash for shareholders, and in discussions with investors and bank analysts, BT is often under pressure to strip out costs
and limit investment. This it has done successfully. Depreciation – a
proxy for capital investment – rose steadily post-privatisation to a
2002 peak of just under £5bn, but has halved over the past decade.
Exhibit 2.2 shows that net investment in tangible fixed assets has
been unsteady but generally lower in the 2000s than the second half
of the 1990s; over this period dividend payments are substantial and
usually more than £1 billion per annum.

Capital expenditure in Openreach (exhibit 2.3), the subsidiary
directly responsible for building and managing the UK's telecoms
network, tells a similar story of no 'step change' in investment. After
limiting investment in the interests of shareholder value, BT's contribution is to make Openreach, the subsidiary created at the behest
of Ofcom in 2006, into a source of distributable cash. This brings in

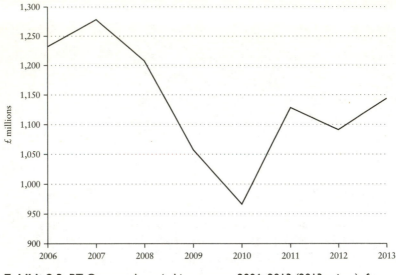

Exhibit 2.3 BT Openreach: capital investment, 2006–2013 (2013 prices), £m

Source: company annual report and accounts

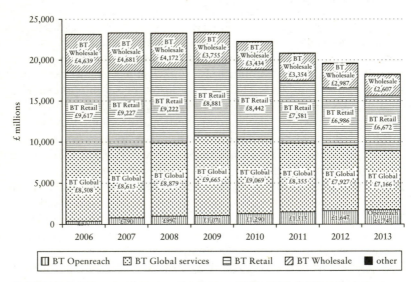

Exhibit 2.4 BT external revenue by division, 2006–2013 (2013 prices), £m

Source: company annual report and accounts

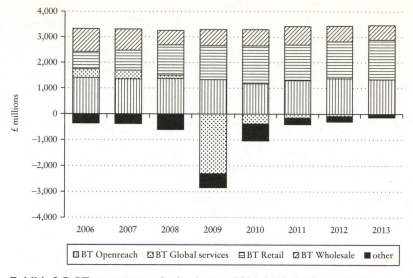

Exhibit 2.5 BT operating profits by division, 2006–2013 (2013 prices), £m
Source: company annual report and accounts

profitable turnover: as exhibit 2.4 shows, Openreach grew from a small base but it is the only division of BT which has achieved consistent long-term growth of external revenues.

As exhibit 2.5 shows, Openreach also provides the second largest and most reliable contribution to BT's operating profits, well above £1bn per year since its creation, with consistently the best operating margin of any BT division (exhibit 2.6). These profits are in part politically constructed since the prices Openreach can charge are regulated by Ofcom as it attempts to balance inducements for BT competitors with a level of return on capital which encourages BT to invest.

The new fibre network is particularly contentious because Ofcom has opted not to control prices: in 2013 BT charged roughly double for wholesale fibre access what it charges for its 9m unbundled copper lines (Ofcom 2013b). In May 2013 TalkTalk submitted a complaint to Ofcom accusing BT of not providing a large enough margin between the BT Retail sale price for fibre-optic broadband and the wholesale network access price – amounting to 'an abusive margin squeeze' (Thomas 2013; Ofcom 2013c).

Ofcom's response makes concessions to BT's critics but also indicates a significant relaxing of the regulatory pressure on the company. In summer 2013, Ofcom announced proposals designed to make life

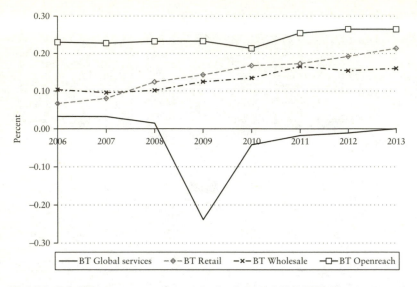

Exhibit 2.6 BT operating profit margins by division, 2006–2013, %

Source: company annual report and accounts

easier for BT's fibre customers – cutting customer switching fees and reducing minimum contract lengths – but crucially has signalled it will not control fibre access prices for the next two to three years at least (Ofcom 2013d). In relation to the copper network, Ofcom has proposed to significantly slow the pace of price cuts for wholesale line rental (WLR) and LLU, Openreach's two key products (Ofcom 2013b). This gentler approach to BT Openreach indicates a subtle but significant departure from the logic of telecoms regulation over recent decades. Lurking behind it is an investment problem: Ofcom are attempting to coax BT by relaxing price controls and easing price reductions, so that BT has the margins and cash to invest. As in 1981, investment shortfalls have forced officials into a rethink, but the outcome this time is the supporting of a large listed multinational in control of a private monopoly infrastructure by an organisation founded to limit its market power. This reflects the state's lack of options, as we can see from the parallel process of incentivising rural broadband.

Rural broadband: BT has government over a barrel

The limits on what the private sector is prepared to do has forced the state back into the business of directly funding telecoms infrastructure. Framing the problem of rural under-provision as market failure, the Department for Culture, Media and Sport in 2010 launched Broadband Delivery UK (BDUK). Rural local authorities and the devolved administrations representing the population left out of BT's 'superfast' future were required to manage a procurement process for a next generation access network for their area. Companies offering the cheapest and best infrastructure would be paid via a gap funding model, whereby public money supplements investment from the contractor, in order to produce an acceptable level of return. This public money is, according to the National Audit Office (NAO), currently expected to total around £1.2bn, with £530m of this from central government and additional funds supplied by local authorities (NAO 2013, p. 13). The plans were finalised in the post-election heyday of the Coalition's 'big society' localism agenda, with the scheme expected to encourage local participation over central planning. Smaller, independent providers were expected to flourish and to offer a range of technological solutions suited to the locality.

The outcome has been the opposite. Smaller bidders complained early on about BT's unfair advantages – its existing network, its balance sheet strength and its engineering resources. By running multiple small tenders, BDUK shut out larger companies too, thereby reducing the opportunity for economies of scale. 'Fujitsu don't get out of bed for less than one million households and we only have half a million', a Cumbria County Council spokeswoman told the BBC (BBC 2012b). Claiming it was anticipating a payback period of 12 years for new fibre infrastructure, BT quickly emerged as the only competitive player. Of eight other companies that qualified to submit tenders, all had dropped out by 2013.

BDUK effectively turned into a vehicle for entrenching BT's monopoly powers via its chosen technological solution; worse still, by summer 2013 it was running late. Only four of 44 projects were expected to be completed by May 2015, the original target. Meanwhile, of the 26 contracts signed by June 2013, private sector (BT) investment accounted for just 23% of total project funding: the Department for Culture Media and Sport (DCMS) had estimated this would be 36% in 2011, meaning overall BT would pay £207m less than DCMS had modelled in 2011 (NAO 2013). Competition was supposed to ensure bids reflected a good deal for the taxpayer. However, with only one bidder, the responsibility for checking value for money has fallen to ill-equipped councils.

The NAO also highlighted serious transparency problems, noting BT was allowed to bid after passing the DCMS' transparency assessment with the minimum possible score. DCMS required bidders to submit forecast costs, but BT declined, citing commercial sensitivity, thus leaving the government 'reliant on self-certification from BT as it was not able to negotiate inspection rights' (NAO 2013, p. 7). 'Securing value for money from the Programme' the NAO said, 'will depend on scrutiny of hundreds of thousands of invoices and follow-up analysis on take-up rates' (2013, p. 9). Questions have been raised about discrepancies between the costs of BT's fibre-optic trial network in Northern Ireland and BDUK delivery prices; an official who leaked DCMS briefing documents concerning BT overcharging for the process by as much as £500m was sacked in late 2012 (Garside 2012a).

A critical House of Commons Committee report in September 2013, and comments from its chair Margaret Hodge that BT had 'fleeced' taxpayers, forced the company to defend itself publicly over the issue (House of Commons Public Accounts Committee 2013b; BBC 2013a). Prior to that it had been accumulating criticisms from other quarters without gaining the full attention of the national media. Independent rural broadband initiatives seeking support from DEFRA's £20m Rural Community Broadband Fund have accused BT of obstructing their efforts by refusing to disclose network locations (Br0ken T3l3ph0n3 2013; Independent Networks Cooperative Association 2013; Willcox 2012; Willcox and Coope 2013). Efforts by the government to use £150m of state money to create enhanced superfast broadband access in 10 of the UK's major cities (Department for Culture, Media and Sport 2012) were scuppered by legal action from Virgin and BT. Having received the green light from an EU state aid assessment, Birmingham City Council's plans to build its own £10m fibre network around an enterprise zone in the city centre was hampered by a state aid complaint from the two companies, the former calling it a 'dangerous precedent' that would 'discourage commercial investment' (Garside 2012b; Leach 2012). This unusual corporate alliance was dubbed by the chief executive of Birmingham City Council, Stephen Hughes, as 'the two oligarchs' (Hughes 2013). The proposal was dropped in 2013 by government in favour of a voucher scheme to help small businesses buy products from existing providers (Williams 2013). Hughes (2013) described this as allowing 'BT and Virgin to charge monopoly prices to SMEs, which offset the high cost with the voucher. Instead of providing a cheap network we are subsidising two huge corporations to give the appearance of lower entry costs'.

Questions remain both about the accountability of BT's use of public money, and its apparent successes in preventing other operators accessing it. However the common interest of the DCMS, local councils and BT in the appearance of success and minimisation of further embarrassment imply that the process will continue unhindered (House of Commons Public Accounts Committee 2013a). With Virgin unwilling to expand, BT will gain a 'superfast' monopoly infrastructure in 50% of the UK. While the company is forced to provide potential rivals access to its physical infrastructure (ducts and poles) to lay their own networks, the economics remain unattractive for various reasons. Technology enabling 'unbundling' similar to LLU in copper is as yet unavailable, so competitors cannot offer a differentiated product. TalkTalk and BSkyB are already aggressively promoting fibre internet to their customers as a means of upselling – a win-win for BT as it generates higher wholesale revenues while reducing pricing pressures.

While politicians may lose sleep over BT not spending enough on fibre, investors have the opposite concern and ask anxiously about progress in cost cutting and winding the programme down. Barclays estimates that BT has cut over £4.7bn from its cost base in recent years, and billions more are expected (Patrick *et al.* 2013; Dellis *et al.* 2013; Sidney 2013). With the end of the fibre programme in a few years, they expect BT group capital expenditure to fall from £2.4bn to £2bn. At present, with customer uptake still low and capital expenditure around £400m per year, they estimate Openreach to be making a £300m loss on superfast broadband. However, this could become positive cashflow, estimated by Barclays to be £300m per annum by 2017 once penetration hits BT's 15-20% target – a target which, given present growth in customer uptake and moves to market the product by TalkTalk and BSkyB, seems conservative, as BT themselves have suggested (Thomson Reuters 2013). If uptake reaches 40% – the level beyond which Ofcom wholesale price regulation would likely kick in – Barclays believes the infrastructure will generate an extra £1bn in operating free cash flow for BT per year (Roch 2013). While taxpayers may feel aggrieved, for BT shareholders BDUK could turn out to be excellent news. Even if that is not the case, and such estimates turn out to be overblown (though the optimism is not exclusively the preserve of Barclays) the important point is that they highlight the expectations placed upon the company: far more frequently than it stands in front of a hostile Public Accounts Committee, BT must stand in front of shareholder representatives and analysts, and explain what it is doing to squeeze more cash from its network.

One way of understanding the rural broadband debacle is as a series of auctions where only one (rather uninterested) bidder turns up, and an attempt to provoke competition produces the opposite. The 2000 auction of 3G mobile phone spectrum provides an interesting counter-example, as a bidding process that was much more successful in attracting a crowd but produced a different set of problems. As with the land on which to build a physical network, the electromagnetic spectrum is a scarce resource, and prior to liberalisation beginning in the 1980s it was state controlled. Subsequently regulators sought to put it into private hands and engineer a competitive market. 2G licenses were awarded via a 'beauty contest' system, with government giving away spectrum based on operator's business plans (Binmore and Klemperer 2002, pp. 78–9). For 3G, the government used an auction system, viewed as a more efficient means of allocating spectrum. Economists who designed the auction reflected that a major design difficulty was balancing 'engineering concerns about the higher quality of service made possible by issuing large licences [i.e. fewer operators] ... [with] ... an appreciation of the benefits to consumers of the increased competition made possible by the issuing of a smaller number of licenses' (Binmore and Klemperer 2002, p. 82). Carried out at the height of the dot-com boom, the auction drew unexpectedly large bids from 13 candidates through 150 rounds of bidding, and provided the Treasury with a £22.3bn windfall (against an expected take of £1bn – £5bn) (BBC 2000). This was then the largest auction to have taken place, and was later deemed (by its economist designers) to be one of Europe's most successful telecoms bidding processes (Binmore and Klemperer 2002).

However success yielded unintended consequences as the telecoms companies were saddled with debt and, with the continued deflation of the dot com bubble, their share prices plummeted and pressures mounted (exacerbated by uncertainties over uptake and lifespan of the technology) to control capital expenditure. BT sold its mobile arm, O2, in an effort to strengthen its balance sheet. The auction's architects argued at the time that winning bidders were under pressure to recoup costs, necessitating follow-on investment, and that four of the five bidders had raised finance for 3G infrastructure the following year (Binmore and Klemperer 2002, p. 79). In retrospect, the auction delivered point value for the Treasury, which used the windfall to pay down the national debt with none retained to improve mobile networks. Significantly, it did not ultimately deliver a decent universal infrastructure: a decade after the auction, the existence of large 3G 'not-spots' covering 13% of UK postcodes and 24% of the land area, remained a headache for government and the regulator (Commission for Rural Communities 2010a). Subsequent attempts to cajole the big four mobile operators to extend their coverage were more carrot than stick, in 2010 government transformed their 25 year 3G licences to an indefinite duration, while raising the minimum coverage obligation from 80% to 90% (Ofcom 2013f). The following year the Government pledged £150m of public money to improve coverage for 6m people living in rural areas (compared to the £500m estimate from the Communications Consumer Panel) (BBC 2011a).

During this time Ofcom was planning the auction for 4G spectrum, which was delayed from 2009 to early 2013. While the leap in technology was not equivalent to that of 3G, there was frustration around the delay because it was expected that mobile providers' 4G coverage could help compensate for the slow roll out of next generation fixed-line broadband. The cause was not technical difficulties but a series of complaints and legal threats from mobile operators over which elements of their 2G spectrum they could repurpose for 4G, with each attempting to shape allocations for maximum benefit. The chair of the Culture, Media and Sport select committee noted in 2011 the difficulties for Ofcom 'adjudicating between competing and polarised interest', amid 'constant disagreement and special pleading from the four mobile network operators' (House of Commons Committee for Culture, Media and Sport 2011; BBC 2011b).

When the auction results were announced in February 2013, the £2.3bn windfall was well below predictions. An Ofcom spokesperson was quoted in the press afterwards as saying that the auction was about maximising competition, not revenue (Arthur 2013). If that were the case, the sale was a double failure. As in 2000, five spectrum allocations were auctioned, with one reserved for a new entrant. Rather than diversifying the market, the incumbents retained their positions with the new entrant, Niche Spectrum Ventures, a subsidiary of BT that does not plan to use the spectrum for a mobile phone network but instead augment their parent's fibre broadband network. One provider (O2) was left with the obligation of extending coverage to 98% of UK households, the reasoning being that this would force other providers to follow suit and build a larger network.

The 3G, 4G and BDUK bidding processes illustrate the difficulties in attempts to craft a competitive market out of a network utility which must still serve the public interest. Competition requires fragmentation and results in crowding around urban areas and rural under-provision. Add in risk-averse corporates focused on cost recovery and shareholder value, and the outcome is inevitably dysfunctional. As the next section argues, in the case of broadband these shareholder value pressures contribute to a form of competition based on confusion marketing of bundled products that attempt to limit process of commoditisation and price competition.

Competition and football rights

The immediate concern of telecoms companies is to gain market share from rivals, prevent existing customers leaving and sell them more expensive products. Hence, the most important developments in the sector in recent years have been the proliferation of complex, confusingly-priced product bundles and a sports content bidding war whereby BT spends similar amounts on football as it does on its fibre-optic network. If the goal of regulation since 1991 has been to drive telecoms products down the route of commoditisation, bundling represents the countermove by industry to limit competition and squeeze more from customers. As exhibit 2.7 shows, broadband has been a growing source of revenue in a stagnant telecoms market where spending on fixed line services has been falling steadily for many years. However, the cost of broadband has been decreasing with LLU competition, with the average revenue per broadband user falling from £16.90 per month in 2006 to £13.70 per month in 2011.

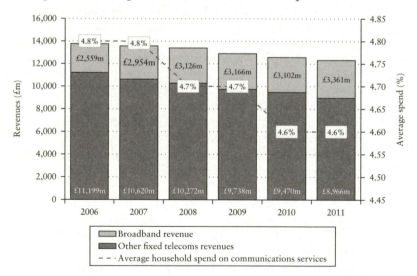

Exhibit 2.7 Composition of the UK fixed telecoms market revenues, with average household expenditure on communication services, 2006–2011

Source: Ofcom (2013a)

	Customer additions 000s	Customer disconnects 000s	Net additions/ disconnects 000s	Closing customers (Q4) 000s	Total Group RGUs (Q4) Units	Net RGU additions Additions	Cable ARPU £
2007	858	938	–80	4,775	11,691	663	169
2008	757	748	9	4,755	12,410	712	168
2009	739	722	18	4,773	13,034	673	175
2010	824	748	77	4,800	13,608	574	185
2011	809	803	5	4,806	13,934	326	189

Exhibit 2.8 Virgin Media cable customer churn, 2007–2011

Note: Net RGU = Revenue Generating Units. ARPU = average revenue per user

Source: company annual report and accounts

An added problem for companies is coping with customer churn. Taking Virgin Media as an example (exhibit 2.8), around 15% of cable customers leave or sign on each year.

The response from Virgin and others is aggressive marketing campaigns focusing, firstly, on claims about average or expected (not actual) broadband speeds and, secondly, on innovatively priced 'bundles' combining broadband, fixed line phones, mobile phone and television. If this works, the key metric of average revenue per user (ARPU) rises and customer switching declines, even if overall customer numbers do not increase. These bundles are growing in popularity (exhibit 2.9), but the downside is opacity: for customers, value for money assessment means weighing up contract lengths, activation fees, line rental charges, call minute allowances, data allowances, upload and download speeds, film, sport and entertainment packages, and more besides.

The best tool for driving up ARPU and reducing customer churn is pay TV, a service that also encourages subscriptions to 'superfast' broadband. Sky has an advantage in simply converting its 11m TV customers to ultra-cheap broadband and telephone, but it is also launching internet-based Now TV. Alongside Virgin's Tivo, TalkTalk and BT recently launched their YouView web TV service, but BT has been the most ambitious. Sky's TV customer base represents about two-thirds of pay TV subscriptions and produces a revenue stream of almost £6bn per year (BSkyB 2013). Rivalling Sky in sport is an obvious way to capture a significant proportion and BT committed £738m on securing premier league football content in an inflated bidding war with Sky in 2012. Its November

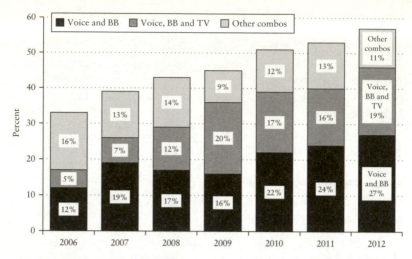

Exhibit 2.9 Proportion of broadband customers using bundled services, 2006–2012 (%)

Source: Ofcom

Public subsidy to BT for superfast broadband provision in the 'final third'	£1.2bn
Amount committed by BT to 2016 for rights to show 38 Premier League football matches per season	£738m
Amount committed by BT to show three seasons of UEFA Champions League football	£897m
Price increase on previous round of Premier League football tendering	40%
Cost per hour of Premier League football	£4m

Exhibit 2.10 BT expenditure on Premier League football, compared with 'final third' broadband coverage

Source: BT annual report and accounts; National Audit Office

2013 acquisition of exclusive champions' league football broadcasting rights from 2015 will come at an annual cost of around £299m (exhibit 2.10) – a similar amount to the £300m to £400m spent annually on 'superfast' broadband infrastructure at present. The rationale is straightforward. Since launching BT sport, BT's line loss rates have fallen to the lowest levels in 5 years, and the company has credited it with the recent reversal of falling consumer revenue (BT 2014b). These significant expenditures raise questions about what kind of company is now responsible for stewardship of a vital piece of national infrastructure in the form of the broadband network.

Conclusion

Privatisation of fixed line telecoms in the UK has delivered a system in which the private and public interests are only partially aligned in relation to provision of broadband. Competition in broadband delivers wide consumer choice (though as in supermarkets, and banking, the vast majority of people use one of four major providers) and the appearance of low prices; it succeeds on its own terms, but it cannot deliver on the promise of infrastructure investment. Margaret Hodge, chair of the Public Accounts Committee labelled BT's activity in rural broadband as 'fleecing' the taxpayer (BBC 2013a; House of Commons Public Accounts Committee 2013b) and there is justifiable outrage about the state of the UK's broadband infrastructure. However, this was the inevitable, if unintended, outcome of generating a model of competition based on driving down rental access costs to a legacy monopoly infrastructure owned by a shareholder value-driven corporation. In a few years' time, the UK may well be left with an inadequate fibre infrastructure which nonetheless generates huge amounts of cash for BT shareholders. Similar to the railways and energy, cross subsidy and state subvention have not disappeared from telecoms: but these are now used for private gain rather than public good. BT's dividend payments (totalling £9.2bn over the last 10 years) and spending on sports content, alongside the wasteful duplication of Virgin and LLU, demonstrates that there is private capital to spare. However, new infrastructure provision in low-density areas will have to be funded by the state, as will widespread provision of FTTP networks, as it is in other countries.

In the 1970s Post Office Telecom's problems were known: the organisation could be forced to disclose its costs, make itself publicly accountable, and adopt new strategies according to the public interest. Now, there is no such capacity for aligning interests even though Ofcom and EU regulation intervenes in all aspects of the industry from pricing to service quality. This is ironic given that one of the original arguments for privatisation was that public sector intervention in a nationalised industry had disrupted the pricing mechanism and markets, which alone could generate rational incentives and outcomes. The subsequent interventions by economist planners are far less effective than the abstract "market" and add new confusions about ends and means. The intention of the regulators is to create something which looks and behaves like a market, in the expectation that this will deliver the public good. However, the outcome is a simulacrum of capitalism which serves sheltered private interests. The insoluble regulatory dilemma is whether to make conditions for market participants difficult in order to drive lower prices, and thus discourage investment; or to make conditions easier in the hope that BT or another operator will decide to build a comprehensive high quality national broadband network.

Notes to Chapter 2

1 Ofcom's estimate for May 2013 is 14.7mbps as an average of speeds for the UK, up from 3.6mbps in 2008, with a 9.9Mbps average for rural areas and 26.4Mbps for urban areas (Ofcom 2013e). Research by the consumer group uSwitch (based on 1.4 million customer tests) found significantly lower speeds than Ofcom (uSwitch 2013).
2 The company does not release details of the financial performance of its broadband operations. However, it says in its 2012 annual report that the largest contributor to a £34m growth in capital expenditure to £457m was LLU, as BSkyB added a further 388 exchanges to reach 1,956, 83% UK coverage, with 4m customers. Given TalkTalk's figures, the total invested is unlikely to be much greater than £100m per year (BSkyB 2012).

Chapter 3

Supermarkets and dairy:
success at the cost of suppliers

Overview

Individual supermarket chains may struggle but the four big UK super-market chains are generally presented as exemplars because they have for a generation combined adequate profits with low price, choice and quality so that these retailers deliver shareholder value and serve customers. This case presents a chain analysis of the sector and tells a rather different story which is both more complex and much darker. The business model of the supermarket retailers is a point value success and a supply chain disaster because the big chains use their power to pass risk and cost along the chain and take margins off processors and producers in dairy. Farmers protest noisily and with some justification about low prices on milk, but the more serious problems are faced by processors whose share of the retail price has been squeezed to the point where processors cannot earn the profits that the stock market requires and it is hard to justify investment. If the test is market share, the big four chains with 80% of the grocery market, have successfully served consumers. But they do so through confusion marketing with 'special offers' usually paid for by suppliers so that retailer margins are maintained; and the weekly shop with big value packs of perishables results in overbuying and a displacement of waste into consumer fridges, which together mean supermarket prices are effectively much higher than they appear to be at the check-out. None of the sector's problems about power relations and supply chain waste are registered by British policy makers who see only the need to enforce competition without recognising that it is the embedded forms of competition which are the problem in this sector.

Their one-stop shop model is fantastically convenient. And their scale brings with it low pricing, choice, consistency, food safety – notwithstanding horse meat – and it brings with it innovation.
Adam Leyland, editor of *The Grocer* (Wallop 2013).

In 2010 Asda slashed its price for four pints of milk from £1.53 to £1. It is all very well for Asda to run milk as a loss leader, but who the hell is going to pay for it? The farmer. The processor. While we welcome this, isn't it you, Asda, who have…. driven the farmers to where they are now?
Neil Parish, Conservative MP for Tiverton and Honiton (House of Commons Environment, Food and Rural Affairs Committee 2012).

Introduction

These two quotes give the story of the supermarkets as it is publicly understood. As industry cheerleaders point out, supermarket chains have triumphed over independent retailers because they offer consumers low prices, choice, quality and convenience. Among the economic policymakers and regulators, supermarkets are put on a pedestal as exemplars of competitive enterprise, with commentators such as John Kay saying banks must learn the supermarkets' lesson about 'putting customers first' (Kay 2009). Rail operators meanwhile cite their modest supermarket-like profit margins as a demonstration of virtue (ATOC/ KPMG 2013). Negativity about the wider social impact of the supermarkets is publicly voiced by farmers and rural spokespersons like back-bench MPs, who complain that low prices are driving farmers out of business.

This case argues that everything is not as it seems. Retail checkout prices appear low but weekly shops and special offers mean that much food is wasted: from a social point of view prices are much higher but that is less visible because supermarkets have displaced waste from the supply chain into the individual consumer's fridge. Farmers complain noisily, but low checkout prices are often more directly at the expense of food processor margins: from a supply chain point of view the damage to the processing sector is a major issue but largely invisible because processors find it difficult to speak out because of their relationship with the major chains. There is an undisclosed story here which we will explore by considering supermarkets alongside the other cases. The most important commonality is with banking because supermarkets present a similar case of stereotyped competition. In the abstracted world of economics, generic competition reduces margins towards zero economic (or so-called normal) profit; in the specific world of financialised banking or supermarkets, markets are ever imperfect and margins are raised towards shareholder value requirements. The stereotyping is achieved when the major players in the sector adopt similar business models which, in turn, structure competition.

The business model of the supermarkets combines familiar and unfamiliar elements because, of course, each sector has specific supply chain specificities and power relations. The familiar element is confusion marketing secured in supermarkets by special offers, as with bundling in telecoms or free accounts in banking: the end result is that the consumer finds it difficult to compare price and quality. In supermarkets, the special offers are frequently paid for by suppliers: supply chain power relations allow the supermarkets to dominate suppliers, with adverse consequences for the chain.

A further recurrent element is that the official mentality is a problem because the state does not acknowledge the undisclosed story about supply chain relations; instead it frames issues in terms of horizontal competition. Providing the supermarkets win planning permission and avoid collusion, there are few restraints on the shareholder value behemoths of sheltered British capitalism. Three of the four major chains (Tesco, Sainsbury and Morrisons) are FTSE 100 quoted, while the fourth (Asda) is the British subsidiary of Walmart, the world's largest public company by sales revenue. The power and position of the major supermarket chains is built on their achievement in capturing household grocery spend by reducing the share of independents and regional chains. This was achieved via price competition symbolically inaugurated by the abolition of resale price maintenance in 1964. UK households spend £1.15bn on groceries in supermarkets each week – about four-fifths of their total expenditure on food and drink. There is pressure from below by hard discounters like Aldi and Lidl, and competition from above by Waitrose and Booths, yet the big four chains still dominate the sector and will not easily be displaced. Asda, Morrisons, Sainsbury and Tesco account for three-quarters of the market and the largest chain, Tesco, takes a 30% market share.

As a consequence, the supermarkets are among the UK's largest private sector employers: the big four employed over 700,000 staff in Britain in 2011, just under 300,000 of them at Tesco. Only state organisations like the NHS, or para-state companies like G4S, have a comparable effect on the labour market. But their influence extends far beyond their own superstores and distribution centres. Because they are retailers of others' products, the supply chain has an importance here which it does not have in our other cases; furthermore a substantial part of the supermarket food supply chain is inside the UK. Food manufacturing is the largest sub-sector of UK manufacturing sector by sales, with turnover of £62.25bn in 2012. If we add the 836,000 employed in food production in 2011 to those employed by supermarkets, something close to 1.5 million jobs are directly and indirectly shaped by the behaviour of the supermarkets.

As this chapter demonstrates, interrogating the problems of the dairy sub-sector can help us understand something of the problems with food supply chains more generally. This dysfunction reflects not only deeply-rooted problems with business models and industrial organisation, but also with official mentalities towards intervening in the economy and controlling pathological behaviours of the private enterprises, because competition is employed as a generic fix for longstanding problems in the sector. Until recently, government played a key role in minimising supply chain conflicts in dairy. The Milk Marketing Board (MMB) was established in 1933 to put a floor under producer selling prices, protect farmers from predatory intermediaries, and in doing so generate stability across the industry. When the MMB was abolished in 1994 the expectation was that, freed from state interference, markets would deliver better supply relations. However, marketization is a reconfiguration of the state, rather than its withdrawal. The end of direct management for the broader public good was swapped for indirect management via quangos, like the Office of Fair Trading (OFT) and Competition Commission, whose task was to shape sectors to appear something like the textbook version of a market. As in other sectors, food supply has become a simulacrum of competition yielding unintended consequences, and there is confusion about what to do besides 'more of the same' – upholding the market imaginary. But the market imaginary does not have much to say about power imbalances. When the MMB was established, the major concern was the large dairy companies, but by the mid-1990s and following the decline of doorstep milk delivery, the supermarkets had become the most powerful actors in the chain: state control has effectively been swapped for control by shareholder value-driven retailers.

The mechanics of shareholder value

> *Everything we are doing reflects my determination to deliver shareholder value.*
> Philip Clarke, Tesco chief executive (Tesco 2013).

Justin King bows out of J Sainsbury after 10 years at the top with numbers to be proud of. Shareholder return since he took over has been a shade more than 100 per cent, leaving rivals Tesco (81 per cent) and Wm Morrison (25 per cent) behind. Return on capital was a healthy 9.2 per cent in the last financial year, better than Tesco ... Hang on a minute, though. That shareholder return, impressive compared with supermarkets, is below that of the FTSE 100. That return on capital? Same as a decade ago. And investors like Sainsbury no better than they did when he joined – the shares trade on a forward PE of 11, just like they did then.
Lex Column in the *Financial Times* (29 January 2014).

Corporate chief executives like Philip Clarke say their aim is to deliver shareholder value and the public limited company (plc) business model is about how firms and sectors do this. In supermarkets, as in retail banking, the large players are engaged in a form of stereotyped competition which aims to hold or improve margins towards shareholder requirements. The business models embody similar practices, though there are differences between chains in reliance on store format or the significance of on-line versus in-store sales. The aim is to grow sales and capture market share from each other while maintaining margins. This in turn directs competition into forms (like space race or special offers) which avoid margin destroying direct competition via price war, and also avoid any suspicion of explicit collusion which would attract the authorities. This stereotyped form of competition has similar resulting impacts on external stakeholders like customers and suppliers right across the sector.

The margins of the four biggest chains are generally stable (exhibit 3.1). Apart from a dip in performance in the mid-2000s by Sainsbury and, even more so by Morrisons during the decade 2002–2012, the average operating profit margin of the big four retailers fell from 5.1% to 4.6%; this was still considerably higher than the margins achieved by French supermarkets who are often collectively closer to 2-3%. The largest chain, Tesco, has seen recent declines, but its historic record is of 6% margins and the others generally earn at least 3%: collectively, the achievement is stable oligopoly instead of destabilising price war.

Modest profit margins from food retailing are normal but, of course, total profit increases as turnover grows: this has been achieved through adding retail space and aggressive expansion of the chains, as shown in exhibit 3.2. Expansion between 2000 and 2012 involved accumulated gross capital spending of £20.5bn by Tesco, £8.8bn by Asda, £11.7bn by Sainsbury and £5.9bn by Morrisons,

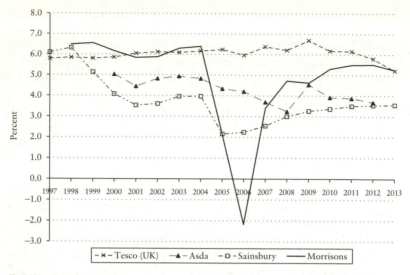

Exhibit 3.1 Big four supermarket operating profit margins, 1997–2013 (%)

Source: Annual report and accounts

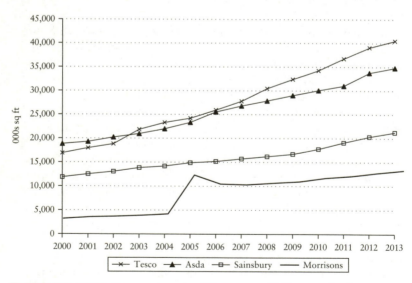

Exhibit 3.2 UK big four supermarkets' floor space ('000 square feet), 2000–2013

Source: Annual report and accounts

including land banking as well as site development. These sums represent not only formidable sunk costs which must be recovered by the big four retailers, but also near-insurmountable barriers to entry for would-be challengers: in effect, they have constructed a vast private infrastructure for grocery distribution which cannot be replicated.

The investment has delivered larger lumps of profit but this is a problem for stock market investors and their analysts because it also adds to costs and does not improve the return on capital or assets in a sector which they think is running hard to stand still. Some industry observers have heralded the end of the so-called 'space race' after the recent announcement by Tesco chief executive Philip Clarke that his company's retail footprint would expand at half its historic rate. This is premature: while the race to build edge-of-town superstores may be over, the push into in-town convenience stores and on-line facilities continues. Despite adding non-food and premium ranges, all the chains (except Morrisons) have fairly static sales per square foot, as exhibit 3.3 shows, especially in the last five years; this sustains pressure to add new stores to ensure growth (or avoid losing sales to competitors). As a result, as exhibit 3.4 shows, capital expenditure as

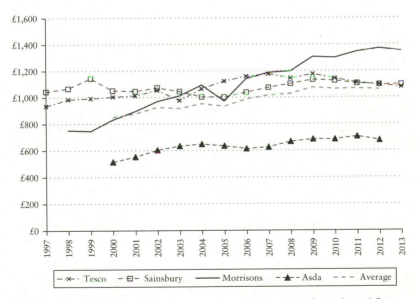

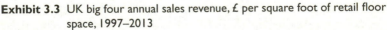

Exhibit 3.3 UK big four annual sales revenue, £ per square foot of retail floor space, 1997–2013

Source: Annual report and accounts

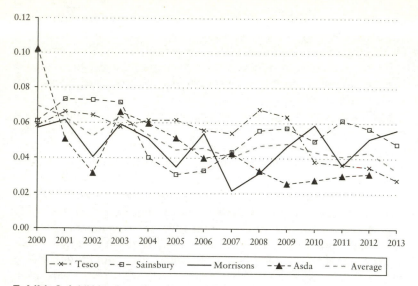

Exhibit 3.4 UK big four capital expenditure as a % of retail sales revenues, 2000–2013

Source: Annual report and accounts

a percentage of sales, a key indicator of expansion, remains similar to levels in 2006 – considered the peak of the supermarket space race.

Taken together, the difficulty in finding sustained increases in like for like sales, with continued pressure to invest in new stores and in on-line retailing, mean that delivering shareholder value remains a concern for the big four whose game always has losers and will end as zero sum. As the quote at the beginning of this section underlines, Sainsburys, one of the recent winners in the competition between the chains, manages to do no more than maintain shareholder returns at the level of a decade earlier. While, this might be viewed as an achievement, the Lex columnist is not impressed; hence, commitment to delivering shareholder value is reiterated by Philip Clark of Tesco, even as his more successful competitors disappoint. Certainly, the supermarkets are engaged in a permanent struggle to maintain margins, as the next section explores.

Defending margins: special offers not low prices

Morrisons hasn't been leading putting prices down, but we are operating in a competitive marketplace and customers expect us to offer great value so we sell two pints of milk for 89 pence so you could argue, why don't

we just charge £1 for that, but in these price-sensitive times, for some
people that would be too much money.
Richard Taylor, Morrisons' director of corporate affairs (Russell 2012).

How supermarkets boost their sales is a relatively straightforward
story about an expensive race to add capacity though different channels (including on-line). But, how supermarkets defend their margins
is much more opaque because it involves confusion marketing. In telecoms, confusion works through bundling which conceals expensive
items within alluringly low headline prices; in supermarkets selective
discounting is a practice designed to manage appearances while
preserving profitability. Margins are being defended by avoiding
across-the-board, permanent low prices against all competitors and
instead making hard to compare special offers of limited duration.
Over recent years, between one-fifth and one-third of all items sold
in supermarkets have been on some form of 'special offer' and the
cynicism of some of these offers has been criticised by consumer pressure groups. One of the issues is whether such reductions are genuine
or meaningful: a recent Which? investigation into 700,000 products
uncovered sharp practices like increasing individual item prices when
placing them into multi-buy offers, and keeping discount prices in
place for longer than the 'real' price (Which? 2012).

A further problem is that of food wastage and the undermining of
menu-planned purchasing which is built into the formatting of purchases around a weekly shop where the trolley includes large packs of
perishables like fruit and vegetables, as well as multi-buy offers which
encourage over-consumption. The checkout prices may be low but
the social price including wastage is much higher. In pre-supermarket
food distribution systems poor process control meant large wastage of
product in storage and distribution. The supermarkets have contributed to rigorous time and temperature control along the supply chain,
but through large weekly shops have simply displaced waste from the
supply chain into the domestic fridge. Estimates from the food waste
consultancy WRAP used by DEFRA in its annual food statistics hand-
book show that out of about 15m tonnes of food wasted in the UK
during 2011, by far the largest component of food waste, more than
7m tonnes, comes from households; retail accounts for an estimated
400,000 tonnes with distribution accounting for just 4,000 tonnes
(WRAP 2011). Moreover, most of the household waste is accounted
for by perishable goods, in particular bread and fresh fruit and vegetables, at an average annual cost to households of £480 per year.

The environmental consequences are additionally concerning.

According to DEFRA, avoidable food and drink wastage is responsible for as much carbon dioxide equivalent emissions as one-third
of household electricity consumption (17m tonnes) (2012, p. 54).
Dairy and eggs wastage in 2010 is, at 8.5%, rather low compared to
bread (32%) and vegetables (24%) and the 17% average across all
food categories; but wasted milk is, according to estimates prepared
in 2011, responsible for the largest single contribution to avoidable
greenhouse gas emissions, at just under 2m tonnes of CO_2 (DEFRA
2012, p. 51, 54; WRAP 2011).

Waste levels in the supply chain as a whole fell by 1.1m tonnes
between 2006 and 2010, according to WRAP. Though this is a
complex area, supermarkets admit the effect of promotions on waste
and over-consumption. In October 2013, Tesco released startling
results of its own studies into household food waste, finding that
65% of bagged salads and 40% of apples were thrown away by
customers. Its response was to promise to end buy-one-get-one-
free (BOGOF) offers for salad (BBC 2013b). Other supermarkets
have likewise responded with claims regarding their reduction of
BOGOFs – which are of course only one form of promotional
activity encouraging over-buying. The fundamental issue is that
the supermarkets operate in a mature, slow-growing market, with
'special offer' competition from rivals and the 'space race' model
of buying revenue growth with new stores facing challenges; under
these conditions, encouraging consumers to buy more than they can
eat is close to unavoidable.

Studies suggest that supermarket business models have also contributed to increased waste in other areas of the supply chain. As one
recent academic study concluded, the underlying principle of supermarket supply chains is high throughput, a constant push through
the supply chain, with waste and process inefficiencies accepted as
a by-product (Bond *et al.* 2013, p. 14). Supermarket competition
has focused on guaranteeing constant availability and full shelves
while minimising inventories, with rapid responses to short-term
demand fluctuations. This puts pressure on suppliers, commonly
related to volume-based, on-time supply contracts with penalties for
under-delivery. Farmers are incentivised to over-produce as a safe-
guard (Bond *et al.* 2013, pp. 9–11; Gustavsson *et al.* 2011, p. 10). In
addition to volume, supermarkets pass down strict requirements for
appearance, with mis-shapen produce rejected. A recent study by the
Institution of Mechanical Engineers (2013, p. 18) claims 30% of the
UK's vegetable crop is wasted by producers as a result.

From the big four's point of view, the beauty of the system is that somebody else usually pays for low prices. Insofar as in-store price reductions are genuine, they are often financed by suppliers at the expense of processor margins. The big four have adapted themselves for the task of margin defence through vertical disintegration of the supply chain supplying own brand products (with partial exceptions like Morrisons' vertical integration in meat processing and Tesco, M&S, Waitrose and Sainsbury use of 'aligned' milk producers). This allows aggressive supermarket buyers to exercise power without responsibility by playing suppliers off against each other. The large retailer's privileged position in the chain as the gatekeeper to the consumer – particularly for products like milk and meat sold mostly as supermarket own-brands – enables them to press suppliers into supply contracts giving supermarkets the ability to drop out at short notice, take additional funds from the supplier to pay for promotions, and access the suppliers' accounts to determine costs of production and how much profit they should be allowed to make.

These are indispensable weapons in the price wars fought around staple 'footfall driver' items like meat, which help expand and preserve chain market share with cheap offers that maintain chain profits. Milk has been the most prominent example. In July 2010 Asda cut the cost of four pints of milk overnight by 28p, with Tesco and others swiftly following the move, as shown in exhibit 3.5 (Ford 2011).

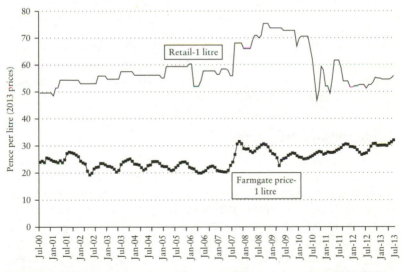

Exhibit 3.5 Retail and farmgate milk price trends: pence per litre, 2000–2013 (2013 prices)

Source: Kantar/ DEFRA/ DairyCo

Asda's Director of External Affairs subsequently explained to the Environment, Food and Rural Affairs Select Committee:

> *[milk] is a key value item for customers: 50% of our customers tell us they look at the milk price every time they go in store, and that rises consider- ably for those who are on low and fixed incomes. It is an important value indicator for customers. That is why looking at product innovation and at ways we can add value through other products is important for the whole industry.*
> (House of Commons Environment, Food and Rural Affairs Committee 2012).

An unexpected couple of fractions of a percentage point lost from an operating profit margin or a revenue growth target at a quarterly earnings announcement are sufficient to wipe hundreds of millions of pounds off a supermarket's stock market value. For example, Tesco's market value fell by £5bn in a single day in January 2012 after the announcement of disappointing Christmas sales figures (Wood 2012). In this context, there is little space for hesitation about the exercise of power to take margins from suppliers. The tragedy is that, as we have argued in the case of meat (Bowman 2012a), this exercise of power is not an absolute economic necessity but a collective, cultural choice of the supermarket chains which are buyer-led organisations. The buyer-led approach normalises the trader mentality and predatory contractualism concerned with point value and maximising imme- diate transactional gains which involve passing risks and costs to others whose margins suffer. As the following sections explain, using the example of dairy products, this behaviour from the supermarkets has consequences throughout the supply chain.

Visible and invisible victims

If market shares are defended by using special offers to confuse customers, the big four strengthen their margins by using their power against processors and producers who have limited alterna- tive distribution channels. Periodically, farmers complain noisily, but the evidence on producer and processor margins suggests that more harm is done to the processors who are both closer to the supermarkets and more inhibited about speaking out. All this is not obvious to broadsheet newspaper readers who follow stories about supermarkets versus farmers, as in 2012 when there was a furore over the (farmgate) price of milk.

In summer 2012, several major dairy processors (including those supplying fresh milk to Asda and Morrisons) proposed price cuts of around 2p per litre in the farmgate price of fresh milk, following a similar cut made in the spring. Processors pointed to a parallel halving in the price of cream – a key support to processor profits – on international wholesale markets. The cuts would have taken average farmgate prices (money received by the farmer for basic unprocessed milk) below 25p per litre (ppl), against average production costs which the National Farmers Union claimed to be closer to 30ppl. The response, led by the newly-formed Farmers for Action, was blockades of processing depots across the country, and threats to pour milk down the drain as a symbolic act of protest. The immediate crisis was eventually closed by the success of the SOS Dairy Campaign: retailers offered temporary premiums, processors abandoned the price cuts, and began negotiations over a new voluntary code of conduct, but the discontent rumbled on with blockades beginning again in spring 2013, this time centring on milk supply for cheese production.

The pattern of political action and reaction is familiar and makes a good media story. Downward pressure on prices meets rising costs of production and leads to farmer protest; outrage follows from sympathetic quarters of the press, with politicians and celebrities joining in to question retailer conduct and supermarket brands; finally, some kind of truce is agreed with, in 2012, a voluntary agreement brokered by government. In all this, retailers and farmers are the actors and little attention is paid to processors. But the issues are considerably more complicated if we remember there are three players (producers, processors and retailers) in dairy all trying to make a profit from the same pint of milk.

Exhibit 3.6 on shares of the milk price, reveals much about dairying as a highly specific economic activity, and about changing power relations in food supply which is a more general economic phenomenon. Firstly, there is the rising share of the milk price taken by the supermarkets. Whereas in the 1990s, retailers took a few pence per litre, this margin rose steadily to above 20ppl in the mid-2000s, and has remained there since. Farmers and processors have both seen declines but, while farmers have been the most vocal complainants, the dairy processors have lost the most: their revenue share of a litre of milk has dropped from 35% in 2001 to 19% in 2011.

The second thing to notice is the volatility. Farmgate prices fluctuate seasonally, and they spiked around 2008–09 alongside grain prices on global markets. The reliance on imported feed pushed milk retail prices up to a high of 76ppl in November 2008. What has

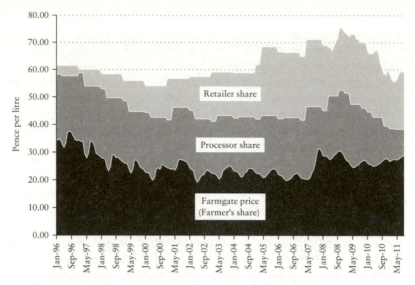

Exhibit 3.6 Supply chain shares of the retail price of milk (in pence per litre) between the main players, 1996–2011 (2013 prices)

Source: DairyCo

happened since is intriguing: retail milk prices have fallen back, but both farmers and retailers have largely maintained their shares, with processors being squeezed in the middle. The silence of the processors in the face of this situation is revealing. Farmers have considerable political and cultural capital as emblems of traditional rural life, and some freedom to speak because they are one stage removed from supermarkets in the supply chain. In contrast, processors – in an industry now consolidated around a few major operators – must fight amongst one another to gain supermarket contracts and are under the continuous threat of losing the contract or seeing the terms deteriorate.

As previous CRESC research has shown, this is not confined to dairy (Bowman *et al.* 2012a). Clashes between protesting farmers and supermarkets, with processors squeezed in the middle, are replicated across a range of agricultural commodities. But in dairy the situation seems particularly odd. The usual excuse for British failure in tradable goods production is foreign competition with low-wage or high-tech competitors. Fresh milk, however, is effectively protected from international competition by difficulties around transportation and EU regulation. Nor can changing tastes explain it – dairy products are still popular. In what should be a sheltered, stable sector, we have witnessed blockaded depots, dairy processors on the brink of economic viability, and farmers pouring milk down the drain rather than sell it.

Farmers: visible victims

Supermarket milk, as cheap as muck,
And the dairies and processor, don't give a monkey's
Selling at a price, too good to be true
Farmers for Action, need help from you
SOS Dairy campaign song, July 2012[1]

While the farmers are not the only victims of the supermarkets, they do have cause for complaint even if generalisation is difficult because this is not a business where most farmers regularly lose money or where restructuring delivers a reliably profitable core. Farmers operate in difficult, often uncontrollable conditions converting inputs into saleable products with input prices varying, weather influencing yield and market prices uncertain. The position in dairying is more complicated because there are several different models using grass and/or bought-in feed for cows to produce milk. The output can be sold as fresh milk which accounts for about half of raw milk production or as other dairy products which all have different prices and exposure to competition. For traditional dairy farmers, weather is important because it influences grazing; but more intensive dairy producers are sensitive to bought in input prices because they rely more heavily on grain sourced on global commodity markets. These inputs can account for a quarter of costs even on the most profitable farms (DairyCo 2012a), and they have been rising for years at a considerably faster pace than milk prices – as have other key inputs like fuel, fertilizer and electricity (exhibit 3.7).

A functioning supply chain would respond to these changes by charging higher retail prices, but as exhibit 3.5 shows, milk retail prices have declined sharply since 2009, settling around 55p per litre – a retail price level which is more or less similar to the start of the last decade in real terms. Meanwhile, there have been massive increases in input costs; farmgate prices, after climbing sharply in 2007, have settled around 30ppl.

As a consequence, the farming lobby claims that many dairy producers are unable to cope with inevitable periodic shocks such as spikes in feed costs, unseasonable weather or disease outbreaks, and lack the confidence to invest in their businesses, or are quitting

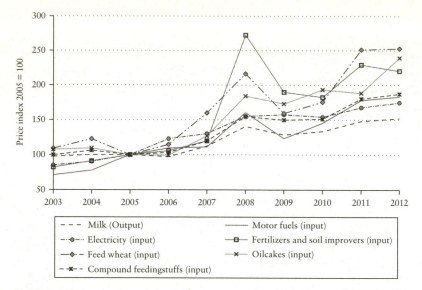

Exhibit 3.7 Price index for key dairy farming inputs compared to indexed milk price, 2003–2012

Source: DEFRA

the industry altogether (House of Commons Environment, Farming and Rural Affairs Committee 2012). Since 1995 the number of registered dairy producers in the UK has more than halved, from 35,741 to 14,793 in 2011. Over the same period, there has been a steady increase in average herd size to 123, as the overall herd has fallen by 19%; this is considerably in excess of the EU average of 42. Milk yields have risen substantially too, pointing towards an industry in which survivors pursue more intensive production methods (DairyCo 2012a).

Larger farms tend to be less labour-intensive and dairy farming – which is the single largest farming sector in the UK, accounting for 16% of production output by value in 2011 – is a provincial industry, under-represented in the south-east and over-represented in regions like Wales and the west country (House of Commons Welsh Affairs Committee, 2013). Some argue that the decline of more traditional farming systems has wider impacts on the viability of rural communities as young people leave to find work, and post offices, pubs and schools are shut (Commission for Rural Communities 2010b).

The prognosis from the rural lobby is dire, but it is difficult to make generalizable claims given the diversity of the dairy sector. Surveys have shown that reasons for dairy farmers leaving the

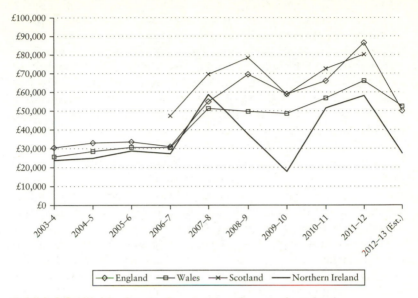

Exhibit 3.8 UK dairy farm business incomes (average £ per farm)

Note: farm business income is 'Total Farm Gross Margin less the sum of the Fixed Costs incurred, before any charges for unpaid labour or notional rent on owner occupied land… In terms of broad definition, farm business income is very similar to net profit as used in financial accounts. The key differences are in valuations, depreciation, breeding livestock stock appreciation and the range of diversified non-agricultural activities included. Farm Business Income includes all inseparable and separable diversified activities' (DEFRA 2010).

Source: DEFRA/DairyCo

industry are not straightforwardly economic: family businesses with succession plans may continue in spite of difficulties, while profitable farms may be tempted by more lucrative opportunities in selling land (DairyCo 2013a). Likewise, DairyCo studies have found neither enlargement nor intensification has a clear relationship with either milk price attained or profit achieved. Those choosing intensification face different challenges about recovering the costs of investment in sheds, milking equipment and pharmaceuticals, as well as hedging feed costs (DairyCo 2012a). As exhibit 3.8 shows for the industry average, farm business incomes are modest and volatile. They are also supported by subsidy. In 2012/13, just over one-third of the £51,000 average income came from farming, with £23,400 coming from the Single Farm Payment. The average hides major variations in fortune, with about a quarter of dairy farms achieving income of greater than £75,000 and around one-sixth running at a loss in 2012/13 (DEFRA 2013).

In some countries, farmer uncertainty has been reduced by co-operative membership, but cooperative participation levels in the UK have traditionally been low. There have nonetheless been two recent changes in the industry which have been welcomed by farmers as bringing added security and stability for many dairy farmers. Firstly, from January 1st 2014 over 1,250 farmers supplying Arla, the UK's largest milk processor which is owned by the eponymous pan-EU dairy co-operative, will be able to join as full co-operative members alongside 12,000 other dairy farmers spread across continental Europe (Mackenzie 2013a). The most significant change in recent years, however, has been the creation of dedicated milk supply pools (often referred to as 'aligned') to supply several of the major supermarkets, most notably Tesco which first introduced the system in 2007, alongside Sainsbury and M&S.

The Tesco Sustainable Dairy Group comprises 650 farmers as permanent members, and 300 seasonal farmers, with Arla and Müller Wiseman processing the output. Membership means farmers submitting accounts to Promar, a dairy consultancy, which calculate a price to be paid for the milk based on average costs across the group (Tesco 2014). For members, it is an acceptance of margin management in return for a guaranteed income and insurance against losses. Costs are audited four times per year and the price calculation is based on a comprehensive range of costs from unpaid family labour and depreciation to electricity and feed; while bonuses are paid for increasing production. Prices are guaranteed for 6 months at a time, and membership of the group is reviewed once a year – giving farmers a degree of security. In recent years aligned farmers have consistently received among the highest prices; in 2012 their own farmgate prices rose, with the gap between aligned and non-aligned farmers widening to over 5p per litre in some cases (DairyCo 2012b). For the supermarkets, the advantage is security of supply and increased control of the supply chain, with the system allowing retailers to monitor the performance of farmers closely, lock-in stable supply at more predictable costs and guide improvements in productivity and quality. Tesco began trialling the system for cheese in November 2013.

Unsurprisingly given recent conditions in the dairy market, the development of aligned herds have been welcomed by the NFU because it gives farmers a degree of confidence to invest in their businesses. However, aligned production only accounted for an estimated one-quarter of UK liquid milk volume in 2011/12, comprising about 17% of UK producers (DairyCo 2013b). This in turn accounts for only a small amount of total raw milk produced, about half of which

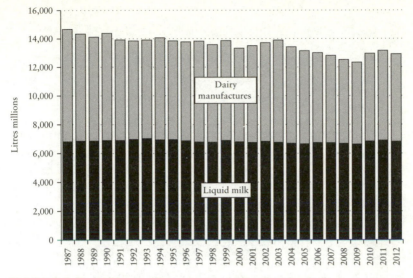

Exhibit 3.9 Total UK raw milk production (million litres), split by destination (liquid milk and dairy manufacturing), 1987–2012

Source: ONS

goes into fresh liquid milk with the rest going into manufactured dairy products, particularly cheese. As Exhibit 3.9 shows, while liquid milk production has been remarkably stable, dairy processing is more volatile.

Unlike liquid milk, cream and cheese is sold in competitive international markets. As in other key agricultural products, the UK's trade deficit has widened significantly over the past decade as imports have risen (exhibit 3.10). Most of this is accounted for by cheese from EU neighbours, and butter, where the UK's two leading brands (Anchor and Lurpak) are sourced from New Zealand and Denmark respectively. This national deficit stands in contrast to the large overall EU trade surplus in dairy (DairyCo 2012c) which represents product looking for an outlet. With the EU milk quota system – originally designed to restrict national surpluses – expected to expire in 2015, the competition is unlikely to become easier (European Commission 2012).

The NFU publicly advocates more widespread adoption of dedicated milk pools, including for farmers who supply milk for cheese, as a means of stabilising the industry for challenges ahead. But, in the light of our analysis, this development would not eliminate supply chain conflicts but redistributed and reconfigure the conflicts to the

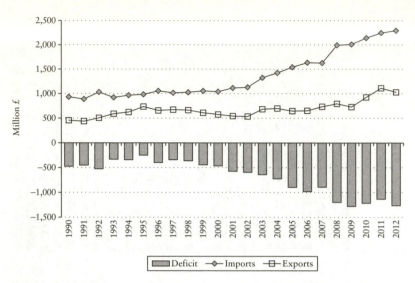

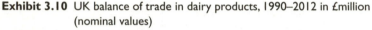

Exhibit 3.10   UK balance of trade in dairy products, 1990–2012 in £million
(nominal values)

Note: the 2012 data is provisional

Source: DairyCo/ DEFRA/ ONS

advantage of the farmers. Aligned pools of producers mean that dairy processors have limited ability to defend their own margins by lowering farmgate prices: Müller-Wiseman already receives around 55% of its milk through retailer-aligned contracts and for Arla this is 26% (DairyCo 2013b). So, while farmers have received rises in the price of milk in recent months, this may have simply shifted the burden of propping up the supermarkets' profit margins away from the farmer and onto the processor.

Processors: the squeezed middle

The standard media story presents the problems of food supply as a dichotomised confrontation between modernity embodied by supermarkets and tradition embodied by farmers. But that obscures the important and changing historical role of food manufacturers. The present predicament of food processors as silent victims of supermarket power is something of a historical turnaround. Until the mid-19th century, milk evaded industrialisation because it could not be transported long distances without becoming sour and cows were a feature of urban as well as rural landscapes (Nimmo 2010, pp. 45–7). The railways and refrigeration brought transformation. Powerful, intermediary milk wholesalers sprang up, buying milk at the station, fixing prices collectively and maintaining monopoly control of separate regions (Brigstocke 2004). By 1917, one company controlled two-thirds of London's wholesale and one-third of its retail milk trade (Nimmo 2010, pp. 48–9).

As in rail and telecoms, the experience of WW1 spurred state intervention. Having already taken measures to boost supply during the war, collapsing prices post-war led to the first attempts at collective price agreements to create supply chain stability, eventually cemented in the Agricultural Marketing Act of 1931. From this, the Milk Marketing Board (MMB) was established in 1933 to mediate the destructive conflicts and power imbalances between producers, processors and retailers (Nimmo 2010, pp. 55–9). The MMB operated from 1933 until deregulation in 1994, with a statutory monopsony and monopoly over the collection of milk from farmers and its sale to dairy processors, on whose behalf the Dairy Trade Federation negotiated. This, ideally, provided guaranteed demand to farmers, protection from the major dairy processors, guaranteed supply to retailers, and stability and assurance that would allow the industry as a whole to plan ahead and invest. By the 1980s, this kind of organisation appeared anachronistic and a lightning rod for the grievances of farmers, dairies and retailers who all thought they would do better without it. Milk processors exploited legal loopholes to withhold supply and lobbied successfully for change in the expectation that markets would deliver fairer prices and force farmers to become more efficient; the unintended consequence was the collapse of processor margins as they were directly exposed to supermarket power.

Following the MMB's abolition in 1994, Milk Marque, a farmer-owned cooperative, was formed to provide a replacement intermediary protection for farmers, partly against the ascendant power of supermarkets. Dairy Crest, the MMB's old dairy manufacturing division, was split off and floated on the stock exchange in 1996. Following further complaints from processors that farmgate prices were still too high, Milk Marque was broken up into three smaller companies (Axis, Zenith, and Milk Link) by the Monopolies and Mergers Commission (now the Competition Commission) in 2000 (Brigstocke 2004). The processors got what they wanted, but the decline in doorstep milk deliveries from 45% of household milk in 1995 to 5% in 2010, along with the rising power of supermarkets, spelt disaster (Hawkins 2011). By 2012, supermarket own-brands accounted for over three-quarters of liquid milk consumed and over half of all dairy sales (Key Note 2012). Having won their direct line to the farmer, the processors lost their direct line to the customer, with prices dictated not so much by 'the market' as by the supermarkets.

As in other food processing sectors, the difficulties subsequently faced by the processors are reflected in frenetic changes in firm ownership, with the trend towards increased consolidation to create a few majors and towards foreign ownership because British processors found it increasingly difficult to deliver the shareholder value required of a PLC. None of the behemoth dairy processors of the post-war era have survived intact. Express Dairies, founded in the 19th century to supply London, struggled with the decline in doorstep deliveries before being taken over by the UK subsidiary of the Swedish-Danish Arla foods, with other parts of the business sold to Dairy Crest. Unigate, once Britain's biggest dairy and credited with introducing pasteurised milk to the mass market, sold its milk and cheese operations to Dairy Crest in 2000. Having survived through the difficult period of the late 1990s and early 2000s, the Scottish processor Robert Wiseman was under heavy price pressures from supermarkets when it was taken over by German dairy company Müller in 2012 (Massoudi and Lucas 2010; Kavanagh 2010). The offspring of Milk Marque are similarly unrecognisable. Zenith merged with The Milk Group in 2002 to form Dairy Farmers of Britain, which went into receivership in 2009. Milk Link pursued a series of acquisitions before a takeover by Arla Foods in 2012. Axis merged with Scottish Milk to form First Milk, which survives to this day. The end result of deregulation is not a diversified market but a highly concentrated processing sector. As exhibit 3.11 shows, three major processors, two foreign-owned and one stock market listed, account for two-thirds of fresh milk purchases in 2011–12 (Keynote 2012).

Long run comparative data on major processors is difficult to construct due to the frequency of ownership changes, but the combined performance of the big three is displayed in exhibits 3.12 and 3.13. What unites the big three over recent years is a pattern of stagnating value added and declining returns. Smaller processors occupying niche positions in specific dairy products fare little better. Mid-size operators like Yeo Valley and Medina are either regularly loss-making or stagger on with miniscule margins.

Predatory contractualism by the supermarkets results in pathological forms of competition among the processors, evidenced by these low margins. Competition centres on the tendering process, in which supermarkets play suppliers off against one another for the right to

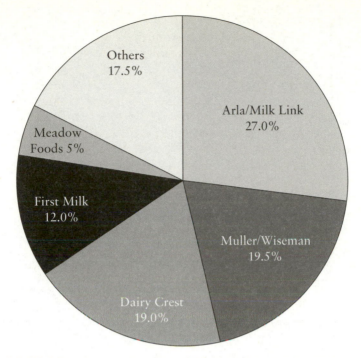

Exhibit 3.11 Processor market shares (%) in the UK fresh milk sector, 2011–2012

Source: DairyCo

supply a supermarket own-brand. Winning market share is a precarious and expensive business for processors: they must not only sacrifice margin but also add new capacity, and therefore winners often face serious difficulties with cost recovery. Supply contracts are put out to tender roughly every two years, and change hands even less frequently (since change of supplier brings disruption to the supermarket as well as the processor). But the threat of switching is real. Dairy Crest, for example, lost a significant supply contract for Tesco in 2012, and, according to analysts, had to accept lower margins to maintain a larger contract with Sainsbury's in 2013 (Lucas 2012). Holding a contract provides little respite. A 2008 Competition Commission investigation found retailers exploiting opaque contracts with suppliers by delaying payments, retrospectively adjusting prices after goods had been delivered, imposing fees on suppliers for wastage, shrinkage and favourable shelf-space, as well as charges for customer complaints. As a result, only half of suppliers were confident that the price paid for milk delivered would not subsequently be

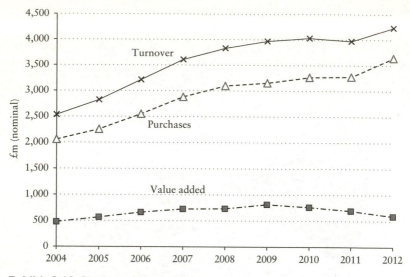

Exhibit 3.12 Big three dairy processors: turnover, purchases and value added, 2004–2012 (£m)

Note: The big three are Müller Wiseman, Arla-Milklink and Dairy Crest. Value added is the difference between turnover (or sales revenue) and the cost of bought in goods and services (purchases).

Source: annual report and accounts

reduced by the retailers through 'retrospective contributions'. This is understandable given that the report found that retailers pressured suppliers to fund up to 65% of the cost of promotions, often at short notice (Competition Commission 2008).

Several of these egregious supermarket practices are now prohibited under the Groceries Supply Code of Practice (GSCOP), which was introduced in 2010 in response to the Competition Commission report. As of 2013, breaches of the code can result in investigations and fines on major supermarkets imposed by the government's Groceries Code Adjudicator (GCA). The effectiveness of the GCA sanction is so far not proven and the fundamental problem remains an imbalance of power which disadvantages processors. Even if egregious abuses are eliminated and contracts clarified, processors will be compelled to accept deals which place them at a disadvantage; and this in turn means continually cutting costs internally while driving down non-aligned farmer prices. Following the widespread adoption of the NFU's Voluntary Code of Conduct, the latter has become increasingly difficult. Meanwhile, competition and capacity

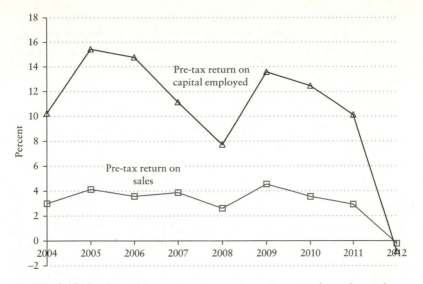

Exhibit 3.13 Big three dairy processors: pre-tax return on sales and capital
employed, 2004–2012 (%)

Note: The big three are Müller Wiseman, Arla-Milklink and Dairy Crest

Source: annual report and accounts

utilisation difficulties are intensifying further due to the expansion
plans of the deep-pocketed, unlisted foreign-owned processors:
Müller claims to have invested £500m over the past two years, and
wants to usurp the Danish cooperative, Arla, as the UK's biggest
processor (Mackenzie 2013b); Arla meanwhile is investing £200m
into a 1bn litre capacity 'super-dairy' in Aylesbury.

Cheese and butter, which make up 27% and 7% of household
spending on dairy products respectively (ONS 2012), can be considerably more profitable than liquid milk and provide the processors
with a little financial headroom. To counteract the difficulties in
liquid milk, all the major processors sell a portfolio of branded dairy
goods, and the most prominent is Dairy Crest, which has 23% of
the branded cheese market and 11% of the total cheese market (Peel
Hunt 2013). The company's liquid milk division has – excluding
profits from selling its property portfolio – barely managed to break
even for several years, under pressure of competition with other
processors, demands from supermarkets, rising farmgate prices and
doorstep deliveries falling at double digit rates. In 2012/13, milk
accounted for 69% of group revenue, but only 15% of group profit,
while spreads and cheese accounted for 31% of revenue but 85%

of profit (Dairy Crest 2013). Cheddar sales growth for Dairy Crest has remained strong, and margins for both the company's cheddar (14.4% before interest and tax in 2012–13) and the cheddar industry as a whole have been both higher and more responsive to production prices than in the case of liquid milk.

This success with cheese was not enough to prevent the Dairy Crest company running at a loss in 2011–12. Moreover, cheddar margins have also been squeezed significantly in recent years, against a backdrop of longer-term trends similar to those in liquid milk: loss of gross margin to supermarkets and upward movements in farmers' selling prices (DairyCo 2012d, 2013c). The industry's hopes for the future centre on exports to emerging markets, but international competition is fierce. Survival in the near future depends on a battle against commoditisation through developing new products which can be sold at a higher margin before they are replicated. Dairy Crest, for example, targets 10% of annual sales from products introduced within the past three years. The implication is that the supermarket squeeze on milk and cheese margins is likely to continue so that branded novelties are the only defence.

Conclusion

Supermarket food supply, and dairy in particular, work on the basis of power imbalances which can leave processors and producers in a disadvantaged position, though (as we have seen) the relations between the players are not completely fixed. Attempts to create more balanced supply chains are frustrated not only by the entrenched interests and mentality of industry players but also by the embedded attitudes and competencies of government. Regulatory institutions and official mentalities are focused on the promotion of an ideal-type competition as a generic fix.

The most significant action taken by the UK government over the past decade to address problems of supply has been the Groceries Supply Code of Practice (GSCOP). The Code was effectively mandated by a previous Competition Commission report which illustrates the limited capacity of official institutions to deal with the complexity of sectors like dairy. While the Commission report highlights the dangers of concentration of buyer power in supermarkets, it is framed as an investigation into 'adverse effects on competition' and its remit is limited to the 'structural aspects of the market as well as the conduct of grocery retailers and their suppliers that might prevent, restrict or distort competition by facilitating collusion'

(Competition Commission 2008, p.7), as set out in an OFT frame-work report (2009) on the role of 'governments in markets.' The possibility that some forms of competition might in themselves be responsible for unwelcome outcomes is outside the field of the visible and the scope of inquiry: government intervention in this and other sectors is geared towards the one objective of ensuring competition.

The GSCOP is enforced by an independent adjudicator, the Groceries Code Adjudicator (GCA), with powers to impose fines on retailers equivalent to 1% of revenue, following the submission of complaints from suppliers; and its sanctions apply to the ten largest retailers with an annual turnover exceeding £1bn (GCA 2013a). The Code empha-sises the need for written contracts with suppliers, and seeks to check the worst abuses of buyer power such as charges on suppliers for favourable shelf space, customer complaints, promotions and shrink-age (GCA 2013b). The government points to the GCA as the solution to abuses of supply chain power, and its creation was celebrated by farming and food processing industry representatives, who had argued for years for an ombudsman in the face of counter lobbying from the retail industry. It is too early to comment on its effectiveness, but there are good reasons for scepticism over its ability to resolve the fundamental problems of power imbalances in food supply. First, it is small and poorly resourced, with funding of only £800,000 per year derived from a levy on supermarkets. Unsurprisingly, the three day-per-week adjudicator, Christine Tacon, said she would 'be adopt-ing a softly, softly approach in the first instance' (Gillandes 2013). Its investigations will be in response to complaints which, while submit-ted anonymously, would lead to the identification of the supplier in any full investigation and therefore create the risk of jeopardising contracts. The farming lobby meanwhile complains that the GCA is limited to investigating only the relations between supermarkets and their immediate suppliers rather than the entire chain.

Second, and most importantly, the GCA addresses effects rather than causes. It is not permitted to consider contract price, only the most egregious contractual abuses. While the latter is necessary, it is not sufficient when the problems stem from structural problems and business models rather than bad behaviours which could be eliminated without solving the problem. Tellingly, the Department of Business, Innovation and Skills (2014) files the GCA in the policy category 'Preventing and reducing anti-competitive activities', where it is straightforwardly claimed that 'Competitive markets are the best way of making sure a country's resources are put to their best use. They encourage enterprise and widen choice for consumers.'

Despite its limitations, the GCA is a positive step because it departs from the more common approach of reliance upon government endorsed voluntary initiatives. More recently, following the milk crisis in the summer of 2012, the EFRA Select Committee recommended a voluntary code to ease conflict between processors and farmers by increasing transparency around price-setting and limiting the ability of processors to ditch farmers at short notice or keep them tied into contracts for long periods of time. This was agreed in September 2012 by Dairy UK, representing the dairy processing industry, and the farming unions, and has subsequently been adopted by most major dairy processors (Dairy UK *et al.* 2012).

While the voluntary code addresses farmer-processor antagonisms, and the GCA covers processor-supermarket relations, there is nothing which encompasses the problems of the whole chain. Instead, problems are divided into a series of discrete markets, with the task of government to devise more elaborate rules governing transactions at a point in the hope of realising the imaginary of an efficient, competitive market. Any form of intervention needs to begin from supply chain specifics rather than aspirations for a generic fix: the focus needs to be on creating stable, accommodating conditions for producers and processors, enabling them to make long term investments towards greater productivity, localised sourcing and environmental sustainability, without the continuous inhibitor of uncertainty and downward pressure on prices from supermarkets. This is only possible if the present structure of buyer-led vertical disintegration is replaced by one which gives the supermarkets a long term interest in their suppliers either through ownership and vertical integration or through long term relations which are not predatory.

Morrisons' vertically integrated supply chain, used for meat, fish and vegetables, demonstrates that it is possible to align interests, sustain efficient processing operations while still delivering low prices to consumers (Bowman *et al.* 2012a). The stability of demand and the ability to plan mean that capacity in Morrisons' processors is fully utilised; with lower labour costs per unit of output (due to higher productivity not lower wages), they achieve dramatically better performance than the other major meat processors, the proceeds of which are shared by the parent company. It also gives the company an ability for plan for the long term with investment and improvements in standards because demand is guaranteed. But this model does of course require capital investment on which Morrisons makes a handsome return because it has the manufacturing competence which other chains lack.

For the other chains, the introduction of aligned milk pools represents a constructive move towards long term relations on an open and less adversarial basis. The system has given just over one-sixth of farmers some protection against fluctuating input costs and the ability to plan ahead and invest with less risk. The system is also more significant than it might at first seem, since it essentially represents several of the UK's largest retailers opting to partially reject market mechanisms and competition among suppliers as the most efficient means for delivering an important product; they recognise that future security of supply depends on social relations. This attempt to abridge the market not only runs against orthodox microeconomics, but against the point value logic of supermarket business models which have used vertical disintegration of the supply chain and aggressive buyer strategies to squeeze suppliers.

The direction of travel is thus encouraging, but the outcome of alignment is less certain than with vertical integration of the kind used by Morrisons. While the aligned herds contract covers current risks (e.g. fluctuations in feed costs, bad weather), the ultimate risk remains with the farmer. Tesco can always change company policy or break off ties with farmers after 12 months, leaving them to recover the costs of investment over a much longer period of time. In addition, moves by supermarkets towards less adversarial relations with farmers still leave question marks about their completely dysfunctional relations with processors. The intense competition between processors in a vertically disintegrated supply chain is economically efficient from the perspective of week-by-week point value calculations of supermarket buyers. But on an industry-wide level it leads to problems about capacity underutilisation and necessitates opportunist short-termism on the part of the processors which can have consequences for wages and environmental standards.

Note to Chapter 3

1 Available at: http://www.youtube.com/watch?feature=player_embedded&
v=HG9Fr02efuo

Chapter 4

Retail banking:
(mis-)selling for return on equity

Overview

The many inquiries into retail banking after the financial crisis have concluded that the sector's problem is not enough competition. The solution
is more competition through encouraging new entrants which will now
be created politically by forcing limited divestment of some Lloyds and
RBS branches. This case argues a different line. The problem with retail
banking is that all the big high street chains have adopted the same business model which has been in no way changed by financial crisis. The
challenge in retail banking is to deliver on return on equity targets in
the high teens despite giving away their core product by offering free-if-
in-credit current accounts and maintaining expensive branch networks.
The now failed Co-op bank dispensed with the high return on equity
targets but in every other way had an entirely conventional business
model which it sought to boost by acquiring more branches. The standard retail response is confusion marketing so that a variety of opaque
charges cover the cost of current accounts and limit customer choice;
while aggressive selling of financial products, most recently protection
products, generates fees that cover branch costs. The almost inevitable
result is repeated episodes of large scale mis–selling, most recently of
payment protection insurance and interest rate swaps, after which retail
banks pay out compensation and move on to do it all over again with
another product. This will continue if new competitors adopt the same
old business model. A radical reform would both remove the high return
on equity targets and introduce fee-based charges for bank services as
part of a shift which redefined retail banking as a low return public utility.

Banks in the UK have failed in many respects. They have failed taxpayers, who had to bail out a number of banks including some major institutions, with a cash outlay peaking at £133billn, equivalent to more than £2,000 for every person in the UK. They have failed many retail customers, with widespread product mis-selling. They have failed in their basic function to finance economic growth with businesses unable to obtain the loans they need at an acceptable price.

The Retail banking sector is not as competitive as it should be. Retail and business customers alike are often denied sufficient choice or access to enough information to exercise effective judgement. Greater market discipline can help address the resulting consumer detriment and lapses in standards, and buttress regulation. Where such remedies can be found they should be deployed.

Parliamentary Commission on Banking Standards Final Report, *Changing Banking for Good* (2013b, pp. 14, 11).

Introduction

The opening quotes, taken from a major UK inquiry into banking, provide three themes that recur in all official diagnosis of the sector. Banking has failed comprehensively to serve its stakeholders: two major players (RBS and Lloyds) are state owned after their distress bailout by taxpayers; payment protection insurance (PPI) is only one example of serial mis-selling to customers by retail banks; and small business has not been constructively financed. There are many suggested remedies, not least because British high street banks combine retail banking with wholesale, commercial and insurance in a 'universal' model. Centre-stage are the 2011 Independent Commission on Banking (ICB) (Vickers) Report recommendations for 'ring fencing' the essential, everyday retail banking services from investment and wholesale banking to prevent contagion during a crisis. But, as for what to do about retail banking, the recurrent theme in official reports and political debate is that there is not enough competition, and more should be encouraged through challenger banks and measures like easier account switching. The opening quotation is from the 2013 Parliamentary Commission on Banking Standards (PCBS) report, which echoes passages from the Independent Commission on Banking report two years earlier. Following recent pledges by the Labour party to cap market shares and pursue further breakups of the biggest high street banks (Peston 2014), the UK's two major political parties have entered a peculiar bidding war over which is the most genuinely pro-competition.

There can be no doubt we are dealing with issues of universal concern where an important public utility is supplied by a handful of private providers. The banks control the payment system, with 94% of UK adults holding a personal current account (PCA). They take deposits from households and provide loans ranging from overdrafts to credit cards to mortgages, and a variety of savings and insurance products. Retail banks are also a major source of external funding for all but the largest businesses. Equally, using standard structural measures, retail banking is concentrated because it is dominated by the five high street chains: Barclays, HSBC, Lloyds Banking Group, Royal Bank of Scotland and Santander account for 85% of PCAs and 93% of services to small and medium-sized enterprises (SMEs) (Mintel 2013a; Mintel 2013b). Policy makers have tried to encourage new entrants since at least the Cruickshank report (2000), but consolidation has continued. Nationwide is now the only sizeable non-shareholder owned player after the wave of building society demutualisations and buyouts in the 1990s, and the more recent implosion of the Co-operative Bank in 2013.

Mainstream narrative about not enough competition fits some accepted facts, but is a partial account that fails to acknowledge the unintended consequences of competition between high street banks. In our view, the problem is not absent competition but competition of the wrong kind, around mimetic business models which preserve high return on equity (RoE) through property-based lending and over-selling of financial products. The starting point is the standard retail banking business model under public limited company (PLC) ownership. This model is some thirty years old and can be dated to 1983–4 when, first, Lloyds Bank set high RoE targets as the basis for delivering shareholder value and, second, Midland Bank offered 'free' current accounts to those who remained in credit. Mimicry by other banks meant the industry was caught in a contradiction between offering high stock market returns and giving away its core product for free (without charging explicit management or transaction fees like European banks). The contradiction contained its own resolution because 'free accounts' were an example of confusion marketing as the costs were recovered by charging, especially for unauthorised overdrafts and using high street branches to cross-sell products.

The model appeared to work for shareholders but was externally limited in two ways. First, the easiest route to stock market-pleasing returns was making property loans, which were easier for staff to assess than business loans and could subsequently generate extra income through securitisation. As business lending skills atrophied, banks were more exposed to asset bubbles. Those banks that fed the bubble in ill-considered ways, like Northern Rock and HBOS, then needed bailouts after 2008. Second, the banks pressure-sold financial products thereby creating a succession of mis–selling scandals around endowment mortgages, personal pensions, PPI and interest rate swaps. Aggressive selling was encouraged by sales-based incentive schemes; this continued at state-owned Lloyds and RBS even after the crash. Sales techniques similar to those used for pushing mobile phone contracts were applied to investment or protection products sold to consumers and small companies. Despite widespread criticism of the scale and consequences of such actions, mis-selling was repeated; after reducing in-house costs by closing branches, RoE targets could most easily be achieved by hitting on the customer.

The dependence of UK economic growth on property prices became an issue in 2013, with a property-based recovery encouraged by government policy; but it was previously ignored even though housing equity withdrawal was larger than nominal GDP growth in both the Thatcher and Blair premierships (Ertürk *et al*. 2011, p. 33). Instead of facing reality, the British continued with long-standing arguments about how the productive 'real economy' was constrained by a parsimonious financial sector. This story distracted from continuing productive retreat and predatory supply chain behaviours which meant the real economy had limited capacity for absorbing more bank loans. The other distraction was the idea that, if banks could not be broken-up, empowered consumers could animate competition (a distraction which also currently dominates official thinking on energy policy). Hence the frequent demands for more switchable current accounts motivated by the observation that few consumers change providers. Banks have been resourceful in making switching difficult, and recent reforms have enforced simplification (Payments Council undated). However, comparisons of the underlying costs of PCAs are difficult to understand. As in other utilities, there is no guarantee that even well-informed consumers will act as homo-economicus, switching accounts in pursuit of minor gains; neither is there recognition that, in utilities like telecoms, customer churn has become another cost of business which only extends the sphere of confusion marketing as companies seek new ways to lock-in customers.

Much of the public outcry and regulatory intervention since

2008 has targeted the pathologies of investment banking because securitisation disasters, 'bonus culture' and libor-rigging all suggest feral investment banks which are, as we have argued elsewhere, 'loose federations of money making franchises' (PCBS 2013b, para. 82). 'Ring-fencing' reforms propose to separate 'good' retail banking and 'bad' investment banking on the assumption this will protect economically-vital retail functions. The reforms would entail higher capital requirements, separate directors, and restrictions on investment banking-style activities. Once implemented, the ICB estimates that between one third and one sixth of the UK banking's £6 trillion of assets will be ring-fenced (ICB 2011, p. 52). The ICB also recommended loss-absorbing bail-in bonds to reduce the need for state intervention once primary loss-absorbing capacity (equity capital) has been wiped out.

All this is very much a political compromise: ring fencing was proposed by the ICB as an alternative to breaking up universal banks, amidst bank lobbying against full separation. Investment banks compete for funding in capital markets and those within a universal bank generally benefit from a higher credit ratings and excess liquidity from retail banking operations. In effect, they get subsidised capital and can operate under lower capital requirements (Ertürk 2012). While ring-fencing might make some difference, it cannot make retail banking safe given the problems rooted in the business model and the limits of regulation. Financial innovation moves quicker than watchdogs can keep up, in a system where products are first released onto the market, then retrospectively assessed. Retail banking is partly about the extension of credit which is inherently risky, but more so if banks are pressed to deliver high returns. The post-2008 preoccupation with making the banking sector safer in the event of a crisis has distracted from the fundamental question about retail banking: how well is the wider public interest served under current business and ownership models?

History of a business model

There have been long standing problems with competition in UK retail banking markets, resulting in competition being both insufficient and misdirected. These problems result from a concentrated market structure and significant barriers to entry, in conjunction with poor conditions for consumer choice, which reduce the threat of losing market share if a bank offers poor prices or service. These difficulties are particularly prevalent in the PCA and BCA markets which represent a wider risk for effective

competition because these products can also act as gateways to other financial services.
(Independent Commission on Banking 2011, p. 197).

This quote from the ICB's final report illustrates how the problems of UK retail banking are framed in the orthodox language of industrial economics: the sector has too little (virtuous) competition arising from a structural problem about too few players, high barriers to entry and poor conditions for consumer choice. However, this raises the point that the core problem of pathological competition would persist whether there were three or thirteen retail banking players on the high street, if their business models were mimetic.

Consolidation and homogeneity in banking is the outcome, first, of pre-crisis demutualisations and serial takeovers aimed at consolidating market share and chasing economies of scale and scope in large 'universal' banks; and, second, of post-crisis state-backed distress mergers when the super-ordinate aim of policy was to prevent disorderly bank failure. The former began in earnest with the demutualisation of Abbey National in 1989. The former building society was bought by Santander in 2004, which also snapped up Alliance & Leicester. Meanwhile, Cheltenham & Gloucester was demutualised in 1995 and bought by Lloyds in 1997; Woolwich was demutualised in 1997 and bought by Barclays in 2000; Halifax demutualised in 1997 and merged with Bank of Scotland in 2001. Two of the banks nationalised after the credit crunch, Northern Rock and Bradford & Bingley, were the result of earlier demutualisations in 1997 and 2000. Following recent problems at the Co-operative Bank, this leaves only Nationwide as a major mutually-owned lender (and it will not lend to small business until 2016 (Goff 2013)), alongside a few niche operators.

The outcome is a strengthening of the PLC sector: for example, the share of mortgage lending carried out by building societies has fallen by two-thirds in 20 years, from 70% to less than 20%, with most of this taken up by banks. The share of PCAs held by banks outside the largest six halved between 2007 and 2012 to around 5% (exhibit 4.1): the ICB observed that the five new entrants to the PCA market between 2001 and 2010 collectively accounted for less than 2% of the market (2011). The market for business current accounts (BCAs) is equally concentrated, with the big five holding 93% of the market (Mintel 2013a). More active competition in property lending has not prevented similar consolidation in the mortgage market (exhibit 4.2).

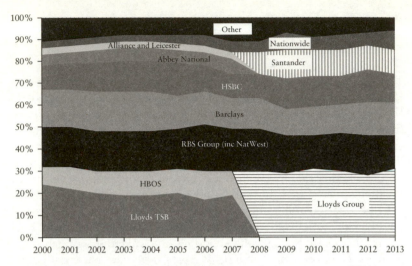

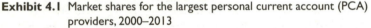

Exhibit 4.1 Market shares for the largest personal current account (PCA) providers, 2000–2013

Note: data unavailable for 2001–02, 2004, 2008

Source: Mintel (2013)

This transformation of the ecology of British banking towards a shareholder value monoculture has important implications. Banking risks arise not simply from investment banking contagion, but from the pressure on retail banking divisions to maximise short term returns for parent companies engaged in a stock market beauty contest. The only meaningful moves to reverse the trend have come from government, not the private sector, and these have been more about adding in new, so-called challenger banks rather than any shift away from shareholder value-driven models. RBS and Lloyds have been forced into branch divestures (316 and 631 respectively) to comply with EU state aid regulations following their 2008 bailouts. The new 'challenger banks' that acquire these branches will represent 2% and 4.6% of the PCA market according to the OFT (2013, pp. 61–2) and, in the name of customer choice, several million people have found their money in a bank they did not choose. The new TSB bank divested from Lloyds, and William & Glyn's divested from RBS, are unlikely to undermine their parent companies' dominant positions, and are smaller than recommended by the ICB (OFT 2013, p. 62). The TSB's £30m marketing campaign (Nias 2013) suggests a friendly 'local' operation nurturing SMEs, but with a stock market listing due in mid-2014 it will face the same shareholder value pressures as

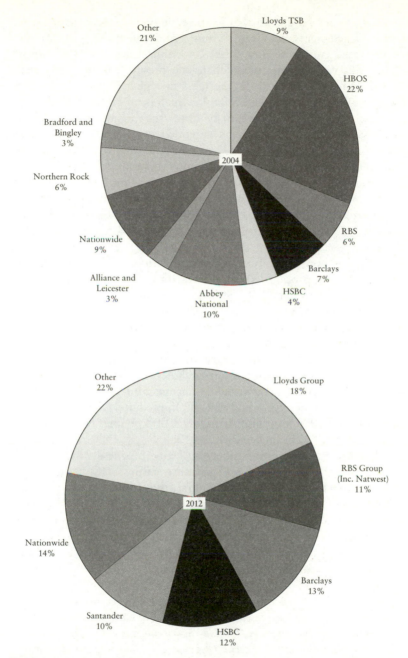

Exhibit 4.2 Market shares for major mortgage lenders, 2004 and 2012
Source: Mintel

its competitors. Added to this is the re-launch of Northern Rock's less toxic elements as Virgin Money, and the quiet, government-orchestrated launch of Post Office current accounts in 2013 (Moore 2014). The only significant independent, private entrants have been Metro Bank – claiming to be the UK's first new licensed high-street bank in 100 years – and M&S Bank, which is an HSBC subsidiary.

These are unlikely to seriously harm the biggest banks, whose business model dominance was extended by the 2013 collapse of the Co-operative Bank, the only mutually owned bank realistically able to take a larger role promoting low-return models. With a 1.5% PCA market share, 6.5m customers and clearing bank status, the Co-op provided a genuine alternative and successive governments encouraged its expansion. However, the Co-op's capacity to challenge for market share was limited by its branch network size. Hence the bank's acquisition of the Britannia building society in 2009, and the attempted 'Project Verde' acquisition of 631 Lloyds TSB branches (Thompson 2013). The deal with Lloyds fell through when the Co-op 'discovered' a £1.5bn balance sheet hole from souring Britannia property loans (Jenkins 2013). Where a state bailout might have followed before or during 2008, the Co-op failed in 2013 under new bail-in rules. As intended, these rules protected the taxpayer, but unintentionally ceded control to US hedge fund bondholders and dramatically curtailed consumer choice. Under hedge fund stewardship, the bank will be radically shrunk and listed on the stock market, which will expect higher RoE. Immediately, it is expected to make around 10% of its staff (roughly 1,000 people) redundant and close 50 of its 324 branches (BBC 2013c).

What are the origins of the retail bank business model, which combines high RoE targets with pressure selling? This can be dated to two events in 1983 and 1984: first, the appointment of a new chief executive, Brian Pitman, at Lloyds; and, second, the Midland Bank's introduction of free banking. In an interview shortly after his retirement, Pitman explained how Lloyds adopted high-teens RoE targets (subsequently reduced towards the mid-teens) by shedding risky business with a higher cost of equity:

> In the mid-1980s, we were earning a return on equity of about 12 percent… However we calculated it, our cost of equity came to between 17 and 19 percent after tax. To make life simple, we agreed, in the British spirit of compromise, to accept 18 percent… . That made us think that if any part of our business was not earning a return of over 18 percent after tax, it might be a candidate for special treatment, and perhaps

divestment... Less than half of our businesses earned more than 18 percent after tax at that time.
(Bose and Morgan 1998, pp. 98–9).

Pitman remained chief executive for thirteen years, following up with targets for total shareholder returns and for doubling share prices every three years. As with many shareholder value programmes, the results were initially compelling but difficult to sustain: shedding businesses and running the rest for margins delivered higher RoE but not long-run earnings growth. This required a merger with TSB, the acquisition of Cheltenham and Gloucester and, finally, the 2000 merger with Scottish Widows. Long before, under investor pressure, Lloyds' competitors had been compelled to follow suit and promise high RoE, and this has subsequently remained the key performance metric for all PLC banks.

The other key mid-1980s development was the introduction of *Free-if-in-Credit* (FiiC) PCAs – a distinguishing feature of UK retail banking, setting it apart from mainland European retail which charged management and transaction fees. The FiiC PCA dates from 1984 when it was offered by Midland Bank, which gained almost half a million personal customers within a year and all competitors followed suit. While FiiC accounts effectively give away the core product free, they also provide opportunities to charge customers a variety of opaque fees for other services. Thus, despite no headline charge for 'free banking', PCAs have been a key source of retail bank revenue, with only credit cards and mortgages providing more in 2011 (exhibit 4.3).

The FiiC account represents confusion marketing on a grand scale. Customers who remain in credit are cross-subsidised by those incurring charges – often more vulnerable customers on lower incomes – through sources including overdraft and interchange fees. The most important source of revenue is net credit interest i.e. the spread difference between income earned on the funds held, less any interest paid out to the depositor: in 2011, income from this spread operation accounted for 43% of PCA revenue (OFT 2013, p. 32). This explains why the flip side of free current accounts is the penalty of low rates of interest on deposits in such accounts compared with ready access savings accounts or other bench marks such as Bank of England base rates: the discrepancy against the Official Bank Rate is given in exhibit 4.4. The cut in interest rates after 2008 reduced this source of profit but overall PCA revenue is broadly stable in nominal terms at £8.25bn in 2006 and £8.8bn in 2011, This is because, as the OFT notes, 'charging structures remain complex' (2013, p. 5).

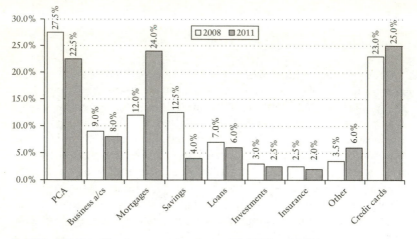

Exhibit 4.3 Retail bank revenue by source (%), 2008 and 2011

Source: OFT (2013)

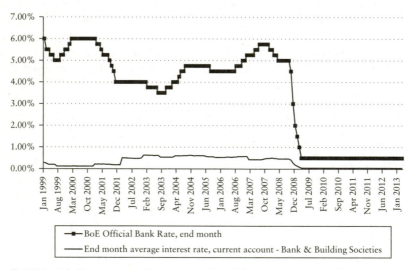

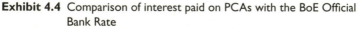

Exhibit 4.4 Comparison of interest paid on PCAs with the BoE Official
              Bank Rate

Source: Bank of England

Overdraft fees contribute most of the rest of the revenue for banks
from a standard PCA, 25% and 21% respectively for unarranged
and arranged overdraft facilities.

Regulators hoping for lower costs to the consumer are playing a

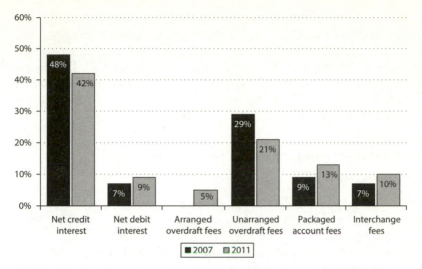

Exhibit 4.5 Retail bank revenues from PCA accounts by source (%), 2007 and 2011

Source: OFT (2013)

Account type	Average revenue £	Share of revenue %	Share of accounts %
Standard	£146	61%	65%
Packages	£300	35%	15%
Premium	£81	1%	1%
Student	£18	0%	3%
Basic	£34	2%	12%
Youth	£14	0%	3%
Other	£118	1%	1%

Exhibit 4.6 Average revenue per account, by type of PCA, 2011

Source: OFT (2013)

game of whack-a-mole because, as old charges are lowered then new ones can be increased (exhibit 4.5). Packaged accounts do not represent any kind of break: these accounts (where customers pay a fee for a bundle of banking and related services such as travel insurance) increased their sectoral revenue contribution from £742m in 2007 to just over £1bn in 2011. Such products do not represent the reintroduction of fee-based PCAs but rather the next step in confusion marketing, as packaged accounts enable banks to generate additional income by cross-selling insurance policies and various unregulated services in confusing product bundles where comparison is difficult. As exhibit 4.6 shows, packaged accounts are a marketing success because they generate 35% of PCA revenue from 15% of accounts. In particular, this enables cross-subsidy of loss-making student accounts, which offer perks in the expectation that many students will stay with their bank.

High return on equity model alive and well

A leading franchise in our UK home market:

- *High performing despite macro environment*
- *Focus on deepening customer engagement and enhancing customer satisfaction, with innovation and technology*
- *Drive income growth in Business Banking and mortgages*
- *Sharpen focus on costs to drive reduction in Cost: Income ratio to mid-50s*
- *RoE target of high teens by 2015.*

Bullet points from presentation by Antony Jenkins, Barclays Strategic Review, 12 February 2013 (Barclays 2013a).

The quote above gives an epitome of Barclays' UK retail business taken from their new chief executive's presentation to investors in February 2013. Antony Jenkins replaced the disgraced Bob Diamond and is tasked with preventing more scandals like PPI misselling and libor-rigging; he commissioned the independent review led by Anthony Salz into Barclays' 'values, standards and principles' (Salz Review 2013) and now promises meaningful change to make Barclays 'the "go to" bank for all our stakeholders' (Barclays 2013b). Yet his presentation was made through the frame of promises about higher RoE.

Jenkins admitted 'return on equity is not yet at an acceptable level' and promised to deliver shareholder value by moving RoE up from 2012 levels of 7.8%[1] toward something above current cost of capital, which Barclays imputes at 11.5%. This promise had a mixed reception from stock market analysts and the press. The *Financial Times* reported the share price was up 8.6% on announcements of job losses, cost cutting and pruning of businesses, as well as the promise of RoE plus a higher dividend payout (Jenkins *et al.* 2013). But *Money Observer* cited City complaints that 11.5 % RoE in two years-time was not enough:

'The 11.5 per cent target return for 2015 will only just cover the bank's cost of equity,' (Louise) Cooper points out. 'So for seven to eight years, the profitability will be below capital cost. That is extraordinary and shows the true cost of the years of excess. It will take the bank almost a decade to recover'.
(Shah 2013).

Of course, some things have changed since the crisis: the cost of capital is currently very low because of monetary policy and as a result, squeezing returns from investment banking has become much harder, so that the 11.5% target is less than the mid-teens RoE performance that had been more usual prior to 2007. The major banks have fiercely resisted a full separation of retail and investment banking because the former's returns are comparatively stable in the long-term, averaging 10-13% during the crisis when investment banking suffered significant losses. For example, UK retail banking made an important contribution to Barclays Group performance after 2008, as exhibit 4.7 illustrates, somewhat belying its more dowdy image, compared with Barclays Capital. From the Strategic

	Statutory			Adjusted		
	2009 %	2010 %	2011 %	2009 %	2010 %	2011 %
UK retail	7.5	11.4	10.6	7.5	9.9	14.9
Europe retail	8.4	−0.2	−21.8	2.6	−1.0	−6.0
Africa retail	7.6	11.5	10.0	6.8	9.0	10.0
Barclaycard	11.9	12.5	6.8	11.9	12.5	17.4
Barclays Capital	13.3	13.5	10.4	13.3	13.5	10.4
Barclays Corporate	1.4	−7.1	−1.4	0.7	−4.1	1.3
Barclays Wealth	7.7	8.8	10.9	7.6	8.8	10.9
Investment Management	–	6.5	–	–	6.5	24.1
Head Office	−2.8	−1.5	3.3	−2.2	−2.0	−2.9
Total	6.7	7.2	5.8	6.9	6.8	6.6

Exhibit 4.7 Barclays Group segmental return on equity, 2009–2011 (continuing operations)

Note: Adjusted performance measures exclude the impact of own credit gains, gains on debt buy-backs, loss on disposal of a portion of the Group's strategic investment in BlackRock, Inc., impairment of investment in BlackRock, Inc., provision for PPI redress, goodwill impairment and loss/gain on acquisitions and disposals

Source: Barclays 20-F

Review presentation in 2013, the intention is that retail banking returns will remain a major source of profit for the Group: targets of 15% RoE in Retail Banking and 20% in Barclaycard have been outlined, and both businesses will be run for market share to deliver mid-single digit growth (Barclays 2013a). At the 12th February 2013 presentation, when one analyst asked whether the high-RoE retail banking targets were 'socially acceptable', Jenkins reply was that they were justifiable, 'if we continue to deliver a better customer experience' (Barclays 2013c, pp. 13–14). On the basis of the last few years, however, the main issue is the extent to which rates of return are affected by fines and provisions that result from mis-selling.

If we consider Barclays UK retail as a stand-alone business, growth targets are lower but RoE targets are similar to those that undermined HBOS before 2008. Formed through the 2001 Halifax-Bank of Scotland merger, HBOS promised a 'strong challenge to the four clearing banks' (HBOS 2001, p. 24) and operated successfully for a time before its 2008 collapse and takeover by Lloyds-TSB. A Parliamentary Commission on Banking Standards (PCBS) report explains that the failure was occasioned by the shutdown of the wholesale funding markets which HBOS depended on to lever returns to stock market-pleasing levels; but the fundamental cause of failure was reckless retail lending as it fought aggressively for market share (PCBS 2013a, p. 144). HBOS targeted and achieved RoE growth from 17% in 2001 to 20% in 2004, which went alongside compound average annual growth in assets of 12.6% and deepening dependence on wholesale funding (p. 7). 'The roots of all these mistakes', say the PCBS, 'can be traced to a culture of perilously high risk lending. The picture that emerges is of a corporate bank that found it hard to say "no"' (2013a, p. 13). The difficulty is that any bank which was inclined to say 'no' to these practices would have been blackballed by stock market investors before 2008. As exhibit 4.8 shows, the retail divisions of the major PLC banks averaged 15-20% RoE for a decade before the crisis, while the mutually owned Nationwide plodded along at around half this. Senior managers of the PLC banks would have been lambasted by the business media and punished by shareholders if they had set their aspirations in line with the latter.

Those like Northern Rock which chased high returns and market share were darlings of a stock market that applauded shareholder returns but did not closely examine how they were achieved. ING analysts summed up the mood in September 2006, saying, 'Northern Rock has managed to transform itself into one of the UK's top residential secured lending powerhouses... We expect asset and

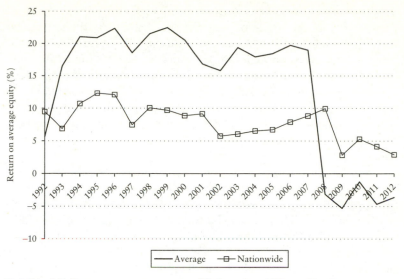

Exhibit 4.8 Return on average equity (%) for major UK retail banks vs
Nationwide, 1992–2012

Note: Comprising UK retail divisions of RBS, Lloyds, HSBC, Barclays, Natwest, HBOS

Source: Bankscope

profit growth to continue to outpace the market, and Northern Rock
is the envy of its peers...' (Sarangi 2006). From the responses to
Jenkins' more cautious promise, we might think many have learnt
little and forgotten nothing.

Cost control and pressure selling of products

*However, a number of concerns became apparent which led to accu-
sations of mis-selling of PPI. These included:*

- *High-pressure sales tactics such as giving borrowers the
  impression they had to buy PPI to get a loan;*
- *Legal exclusions which meant claims could not be made in
  some cases such as back pain and stress, common causes of
  absence from work;*
- *The sale of PPI policies to customers who were self-employed
  and not eligible to claim;*
- *Requirements for customers to opt out of the product rather
  than opt in – which in some cases meant they were unaware.*

(Salz Review 2013, p. 56).

This is a description of standard retail financial selling practices, such as those that underpinned the mis-selling of PPI to around three million customers. It is taken from the Salz Review's investigation into Barclays, though similar remarks can be found in other inquiries about retail banking practices. For example, the Financial Conduct Authority (FCA) 2013 report into the Lloyds-HBOS incentives schemes present detail on the financial inducements for the company's sales force from 2010–12; these continued the practices of high-pressure selling, even after the scale of PPI mis-selling was well-known.

Retail banking is different from chain retailing. Banking requires a back office to process and service products and a high street front office to make sales. A large network of branches is necessary to reach customers. These are expensive in fixed costs, and industrial economists identify them as a key barrier to entry: it is not possible to win significant market share without a branch network. Despite the rise of online and telephone banking, according to the OFT (2013), 78% of PCA holders visit a branch at least once a year. A branch network requires town centre real estate, sophisticated IT infrastructure and thousands of staff. Branches typically account for 75% of total retail distribution costs, and in 2007 the cost outlay was estimated at around £800,000 per-branch per-year (Bradey 2013; Quarry *et al.* 2012; Deloitte 2007). Building a new network from scratch is unattractive without the guarantee of an established customer base and strong brand identity. With the exception of Metro Bank, all significant new retail banks have either received a branch network and a customer base in advance with assistance from the state (TSB, Virgin), or attached them to existing physical premises for other businesses (Post Office, supermarket banks).

For owners of a network, if costs are kept down then small income increases can translate into significant increases in profits, as fixed costs will not increase simultaneously. Management accounting therefore identifies expensive functions to be moved to casualised back office call centres, as the front office becomes a showroom; it also directs the closure of less profitable outlets; and creates a poorly paid and trained workforce using automated procedures for loan application assessments and rehearsed sales pitches with limited workforce understanding of small print. Workers can be motivated with low basic pay so that decent wages depend on hitting sales targets and winning bonuses (FCA 2013). Much of this is standard British retail practice but it is poorly suited to selling technically complex products.

	Inhabitants per branch No.	Revenues per branch £	Annual closure rate %
France	1,684	799,834	−1.10%
Germany	2,142	1,327,816	0.00%
Italy	1,802	850,178	−0.30%
Netherlands	6,686		−7.70%
Spain	1,069	521,267	−2.80%
United Kingdom	6,003	4,355,769	−1.10%
EU average	2,345		−0.80%

Exhibit 4.9 Comparison of branch density and revenues for key markets

Source: European Banking Foundation & Eurostat. Data from Quarry *et al.* (2012)

While branches are necessary, the ideal for established banks with large branch networks is fewer branches that sell more: in 2011, there were 199 branches per million inhabitants in the UK compared with the EU average of 463 (exhibit 4.9). Rural areas are worst affected by falling branch density: estimates from 2009 indicate that 1,200 communities were without any branch, and a further 900 had only one branch – providing hundreds of local monopolies akin to the small-town supermarket branch (Ashton 2009). UK banks also squeeze significantly more revenue from their branches than comparable EU nations, as exhibit 4.9 shows.

Pressure to reduce the costs of the branch network, while increasing the revenue generated by each branch are key elements of the retail bank business model. The PPI scandal provides a telling example of how these processes play out, demonstrating the extreme competitive pressures around selling, the vulnerability of a financially illiterate public to often ill-informed bank staff, and the fundamental weakness of financial regulators who introduce retrospective restrictions on harmful practices in the face of intense lobbying. Designed to cover debt repayments in unforeseen circumstances such as illness or redundancy, PPI was promoted as a small add-on to monthly interest payments, which were kept low as a marketing tactic (FSA 2012). This product was quickly recognised as problematic, but more than six years elapsed between the first complaint and effective regulatory action.

The alarm was initially raised by a 2005 complaint from the Citizens Advice Bureau (OFT 2005). This complaint cited estimates that banks were earning gross premium revenue of £5bn per year from the product, with over 20m policies outstanding after rapid sales growth from incentivised staff; the total cost of premiums amounting to anything between 13% and 56% of overall loan value (Citizens Advice 2005). This initiated enquiries by the OFT in October 2006 and the Competition Commission in February 2007. The Competition Commission found that the average claim ratio was only 14% (most insurance products are well over 50%) and, among the biggest providers, PPI was providing a return on equity of 490% (PCBS 2012a). Reviews by the FSA in 2005, 2006 and 2007 raised similar concerns, but, crucially, failed to provide conclusive evidence of comprehensive, sector-wide mis-selling and therefore could not justify effective action (PCBS 2012b). Meanwhile, PPI was the subject of hundreds of thousands of complaints to the Financial Ombudsman over claims being unfairly turned down by banks, customers (still) being sold products they did not need, did not understand, or did not even realise they had bought (Financial Ombudsman Service 2013). Clive Briault, former MD for retail markets at the FSA, explained the delays thus:

> *Once the problems in the selling of PPI were identified and communi-cated by the FSA… banks should have focused on how they were going to address these problems. But instead they devoted their attention to preserving profitable business through a mixture of denial, inaction, and vigorous push-back.*
> (PCBS 2012b).

FSA initiatives to improve bank practices on PPI, under the banner of Treating the Customer Fairly, were resisted:

> *… in the specific context of PPI, the senior management and boards of firms did not take TCF sufficiently seriously, and at the end of the day profitability took precedence over meeting FSA rules (both high level principles and more detailed rules).*
> (PCBS 2012b).

New regulations restricting the sale of PPI did not arrive until October 2011. With an estimated 50m PPI products sold, the total cost of mis-selling to UK banks, taking into account fines and provi-sions, is likely to exceed £20bn – not altogether dissimilar figures to the losses on some of the mis-sold mortgage-backed securities which were cause for censure of investment banks. By August 2013, provisions for the costs of PPI mis-selling totalled £18.8bn, with the big four banks accounting for about two-thirds – and Lloyds alone setting aside more than £7bn (Which? 2013). The practice was nonetheless industry-wide, with Nationwide and the Co-op also implicated. Punitive measures do not address – or seek – the root causes of this behaviour but instead attempt to ensure PPI sales are more competitive.

A similar story of repeated warnings and lethargic responses is repeated in the FCA's recent investigation of Lloyds-HBOS' use of staff incentive schemes to drive mis-selling, which led to a fine of £28 million (FCA 2013). These banks were the UK's leading providers of protection and investment products and together, over the 2010–2012 period under FCA investigation, their 1,900 advisers sold just under 1.1m products to 692,000 customers. Around half of advisers received bonuses at some point during the period – averaging £1,150, with options to receive bonuses in advance (FCA 2013, para. 4.30). As in investment banking, bonuses for retail bank staff were in effect used to encourage excessive risk-taking with negative social consequences, and were paid with a regularity which muddied the relationship to salary. The difference is that in retail banking bonuses were used to squeeze additional productivity from already low-wage staff subject to aggressive cost cutting. Failure to meet targets could entail automatic demotions and bonus clawbacks which caused some advisers to sell products to themselves and family members in order to hit targets. Subsequent reviews carried out by the banks on 'higher risk advisers' (around 12% of the workforce) showed 54% of sales to be potentially unsuitable with 14% deemed 'process fails', with only 32% of sales passed as unproblematic. 'Advice fails' recognised at the time did not stop bonus pay-outs (FCA 2013, para. 2.10).

Shocking as the details are, the broader context is equally disturbing. Firstly, this happened in 2010–12, long after the banking crash of 2007–09, thereby demonstrating how business models and cultures survived the shock of crisis and the transition to state ownership. Lloyds persisted with such patently aggressive incentive schemes because it wanted to double its 'bancassurance' operation's customer base by 2015, and because protection products were highly profitable: Lloyds earned on average £600 per protection policy sold, in comparison to £60 per premium investment plan (FCA 2013, para. 4.5). Secondly, the episode again highlights the weakness of regulators. As the FCA notes, this type of incentive-based mis-selling, in different forms, has been the subject of regulatory interventions for over a decade, with six separate FSA publications on the matter between 2005 and 2008. Alongside several disciplinary actions against companies in the Lloyds stable over the past decade, in September 2003 Lloyds TSB was fined for target-based mis-selling of high income bonds. Indeed, Lloyds had removed staff incentive schemes (similar to those uncovered by the FCA recently) in October 2004 to meet requirements in the FSA's Treating Customers Fairly programme (FCA 2013, para. 4.110).

The guilty parties of PPI have promised to do better, inter alia by reforming incentive schemes. Barclays, for example, has dropped sales-based incentives and adopted schemes based on customer satisfaction in order to 'rebuild trust' (Parsons 2012). Trust is the operative word because all such measures are voluntary, and the past record of the banks in this area provides little cause for optimism. The fundamental drivers of the misbehaviour are unchanged: the retail banking model is still largely based on free current accounts and high RoE; and the system's regulator can only rule against innovation retrospectively when there is a clear record of abuse.

The great hope is that future abuses will ultimately be prevented not by all-seeing regulators, but by empowered rational acting customers. As the OFT puts it:

> *Empowered consumers drive competition, which puts pressure on providers to reduce the price and increase the quality of services offered. This forces providers to operate efficiently and stimulates innovation for the benefit of consumers and the UK economy. We want to see this dynamic process operating well across retail banking markets in the UK… When markets work well, more efficient businesses thrive by providing what consumers want, better and more cost-effectively than their competitors. Businesses that do not offer products that meet consumer needs or do not offer value for money will either need to improve their product offering or risk being forced to exit the market. Through this process, competition drives efficiency and innovation, thereby increasing productivity and economic growth.*
> (OFT 2013, pp. 11–12).

Within this generic competition frame, after endless failures, the standard policy response is always that competition could work if customers behaved with homo economicus motives and maintained vigilance over prices and charges. Such behaviour is unlikely if, as the Salz review noted, 'various surveys have shown that quite large numbers of people have a tenuous understanding of their own finances and are not well prepared for making good choices of financial products' (2013, p. 29).

This is reflected in official reports. The OFT (2008) found that consumers changed current accounts once every 16 years on average. Despite years of efforts to make switching easier and consumers better informed, not to mention recent scandals, only 3.1% of customers switched accounts in 2012 (OFT 2013, pp. 103–5). As the OFT noted in its review of PCAs, consumers 'still do not know the key costs of their PCA, such as credit and debit interest rates and charges for overdrafts' (para. 57). Three-quarters of OFT survey respondents said they had never considered switching account provider – the implication being that people favour the provider they have over constant deal hunting. Even for the motivated, deciding which account offers best value is no easy matter, as the OFT admits, 'given limited consumer knowledge and the fragmented nature of pricing' (para. 48). Rather than pricing, which was too complex to make comparisons, the OFT used customer complaints as a proxy measure for value. Reforms introduced in September 2013 to ease the switching process (e.g. with seven day time limits and automated transfers of payment arrangements) represent the last chance saloon as it is hard to see where regulators go next in efforts to shape retail banking to fit the competitive imaginary.

Lending on property vs lending to SMEs

'Over the past year the Funding for Lending Scheme has contributed to the recovery by helping to significantly improve credit conditions, especially for households. The changes announced today refocus the FLS where it is most needed – to underpin the supply of credit to small businesses over the next year – without providing further broad support to household lending that is no longer needed' (Mark Carney, Governor of the Bank of England).

'Now that the housing market is starting to pick up, it is right that we focus the scheme's firepower on small businesses. Small firms are the lifeblood of our economy. That's why we're reforming the banks, introducing the employment allowance and now focussing the Funding for Lending Scheme to support them' (George Osborne, Chancellor of the Exchequer). (HM Treasury 2013a).

In a coded way, the Chancellor of the Exchequer and the Bank of England Governor in the above quotes admit that, despite all the generous support and encouragement provided by the state in recent years through 'accommodative' monetary policy and schemes like Funding for Lending, banks still were not doing the right thing. British banks were continuing to focus lending on property in a manner Carney found unsettling from a financial stability perspective, and banks were apparently starving small and medium size enterprises (SMEs) of capital in a manner that was politically problematic for Osborne.

Data from the Bank of England is unequivocal, showing a sharp decline in bank lending to 'non-financial companies' (mainly SMEs) during the 2008–10 period and no subsequent recovery despite inducements to lend.[2] The position in large businesses is very different because these can access capital markets and syndicated loans. As exhibit 4.10

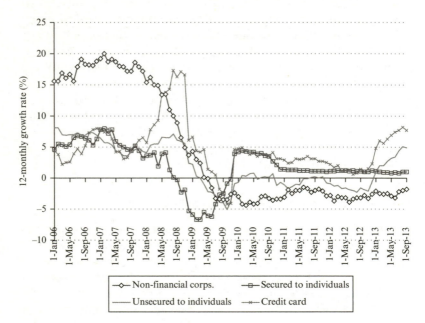

Exhibit 4.10 Monthly 12 month growth rate of MFI sterling net lending, January 2006 – September 2013 (seasonally adjusted)

Notes:
MFI: Monetary Financial Institution, a category used by the Bank of England for banks and other credit-granting institutions
Sterling net lending: loans extended by MFIs in Pounds Sterling minus repayments by their debtors
NFC: non-financial corporation, and the figure here represents lending to other non-MFI organisations
FLS: Funding for Lending scheme
QE: quantitative easing

Source: Bank of England

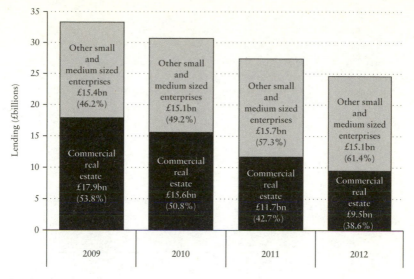

Exhibit 4.11 Gross new lending to SMEs by major high street banks, 2009–2012 (£bn)

Source: Large (2013)

shows, secured lending to individuals (mortgages), and credit card debt dipped into negative growth for only a year post-crisis. Lending to non-financial businesses has remained in negative growth in every month since April 2009; though this is not necessarily a significant decline in lending to the productive economy. As exhibit 4.11 shows, the entirety of the major high street banks' fall in gross new lending to SMEs over the past four years has come from declines in commercial property lending, which has almost halved, while general SME gross lending has remained around £15bn. Overall, SMEs are net lenders to the banking sector: according to the British Bankers' Association (BBA) in the third quarter of 2013, SME deposits at banks of £133bn exceed borrowings (loans and overdrafts) at £113bn (including £12bn of approved overdrafts not drawn down) (BBA 2013).

The inclination of the UK financial sector to lend on house property, as noted by the Governor of the Bank of England in the quote at the head of this section, has strengthened since 2008 in spite of a financial crisis involving a property bubble. Yet, the Bank of England's own data shows that lending to private non-financial companies has become much more risky since 2008, while secured lending to individuals (mainly on property) has been relatively stable in terms of the levels of debt write-offs (exhibit 4.12). A preference

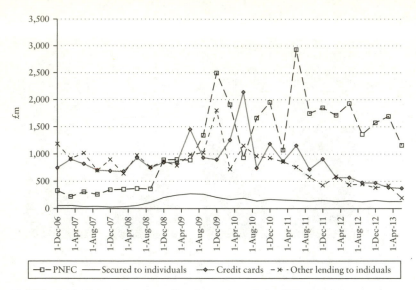

Exhibit 4.12 Quarterly value of lending write-offs for UK resident monetary financial institutions (£m), Q4 2006 – Q1 2013

Source: Bank of England

for lending on property is further strengthened by the way that the simplicity of the mortgage proposition suits the sales system. Centralised credit-scoring systems minimise costs and expertise required for assessments and this in turn allows mortgage approval to be automated on easily obtainable information – the borrower's income, credit history and the property's market value.

SME lending is an altogether more complicated proposition, and the Federation of Small Businesses and the Engineering Employers Federation among others have criticised banks' approach to lending. It has been alleged that RBS, previously the UK's largest SME lender, was actively irresponsible. A report by Andrew Large, formerly a deputy governor of the Bank of England, into business lending at RBS concluded that some decline in SME lending was inevitable post crisis:

> *In the build up to 2008, growth in the SME market was fuelled by lending to the Commercial Real Estate sector, as well as to businesses utilising real estate collateral to support speculative and other trading activities. RBS built a large share in the SME market, largely off the back of real estate lending of both types, often relying on rising asset prices rather than an analysis of borrowers' trading quality to support.*
> (Large 2013, p. 29).

However, there was also some overshoot in the adjustment. Large's estimates of the ability of SMEs to service debt suggests overall SME lending stock fell from a peak of £25-30bn above prudent levels in the first quarter of 2009 (£221bn) to £30-35bn below prudent levels in the first half of 2013 at £170bn (2013, pp. 13–14). Attempts to impose higher credit standards alongside reducing the loan to deposit ratio, 'resulted in RBS turning away some lending to the sector which would otherwise be attractive' (Large 2013, p. 4). In addition, the credit skills of relationship managers had been 'neglected in the run up to 2008' (Large 2013, p. 5): in the more complex, cautious post-crash economic environment, staff lacked the ability to assess business creditworthiness, which is a problem because SME lending cannot be automated in the same way as mortgages.

As well as difficulties accessing finance, SMEs have complained about their treatment by banks. These concerns surfaced publicly in a December 2013 report authored by Lawrence Tomlinson, an advisor to the Business Secretary Vince Cable, which alleges that RBS used harsh interpretations of debt covenants and compliant administrators to engineer defaults among debtor SMEs so that assets of otherwise viable enterprises could be sold off at low prices to the bank's West Register commercial property unit, thereby making a quick profit for the bank's Global Restructuring Group (Tomlinson 2013, pp. 7–8). The FCA is currently carrying out its own investigation following a request made by Cable (Treanor 2013).

The controversy aroused by the Tomlinson report highlights the prevailing confusion about whether banks are a profit-driven private enterprise governed by market forces and run for shareholders, a public utility acting in the interests of customers, or an instrument of state economic policy nurturing favoured sectors. The aspiration, it seems, is to have something of all three all at once: shareholder value-driven business models are expected to deliver socially beneficial results, and private enterprise should heed state advice on lending.

As an alternative way of addressing the roots of this problem, the matter can be set in a broader historical context. From a structural point of view, the banks are not culpably failing society, they are responding to structural realities: there is reasonable national fit between a sales-led, property-focused banking system and a declining productive economy. Manufacturing gross value added (GVA) as a share of the UK total has declined from over 30% to 10% over the last three decades (exhibit 4.13), while real estate and financial services have each increased to 10%; moreover, major surviving manufacturing firms are increasingly reliant on capital markets rather than

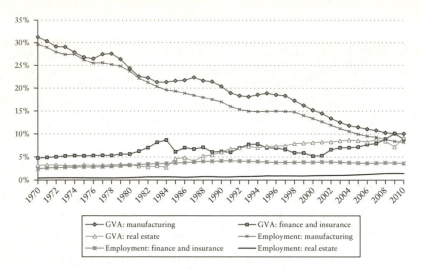

Exhibit 4.13 Industry shares of national gross value added (GVA) and employment, 1970–2010

Note: GVA = gross value added; EMP = employment

Source: EU KLEMS database

bank loans. On this basis, the shift in lending priorities towards the financial sector and property shown in exhibit 4.14 has some logic.

The significance of residential and commercial property lending in the banks' portfolio thus reflects broader changes in the structure of the economy which finance has influenced, but does not direct or control. Nonetheless, policy measures have been introduced on the assumption that finance can lead other economic activities and help to reshape the economy through more lending. A number of initiatives have followed: the government's Project Merlin (where the big four retail banks were encouraged to commit to lending more to business as part of a package of measures) (HM Treasury 2011); the Bank of England's Funding for Lending (which provides cheap credit for the banks in return for commitments to lend to the 'real economy') (Churm *et al.* 2012); as well as the creation of a green investment bank (Vivid Economics 2011) and a 'business bank' to supply credit to SMEs (Department for Business, Innovation and Skills 2013), both involving government funds as well as external sources of credit.

All of these are policy responses to perceived failures of the banking sector, based on an assumption that credit creation will automatically bring economic benefits regardless of the recipients.

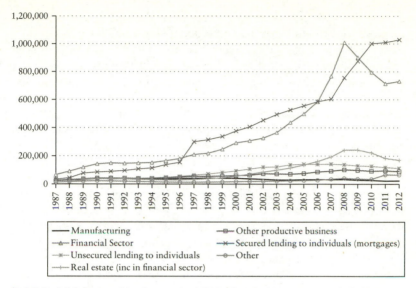

Exhibit 4.14 Sectoral lending in the UK by financial institutions, 1987–2012 (£m, nominal data)

Note: the data covers UK resident financial institutions lending in sterling

Source: BoE

This amounts to a *foie gras* industrial policy – the force feeding of SMEs with loans is as likely to create a German-style Mittlestand or new Silicon Valley as the tube of corn feed is to produce a healthy goose (Bentham *et al.* 2013). The declining productive economy limits the possibilities of (non-property) SME lending, while the retail bank business model emphasises selling over relationships, especially with SME customers.

Conclusion

The reform of the UK's banks has received much attention since 2008. A variety of official inquiries and reports have largely converged on the objectives of making retail banking more competitive, especially through introducing new players (so-called challengers) and by helping customers to switch between providers more easily, and of encouraging banks to lend to SMEs. These objectives reflect significant discontent about the outcomes produced by retail banks but they fail to engage with the business model. Specifically, the recommendations do not reflect the role of RoE targets in the mid-teens as a driver of behaviours and practices in the standard retail bank business model which has also included giving away the core product under the free-if-in-credit current account system. The shareholder value-led model then delivers through confusion marketing, cross (and sometimes mis-) selling of financial products, actions to increase revenue per branch and a preference for lending on property above other kinds of lending. Simply adding competition is no guarantee of different outcomes, if new entrants adopt similar business model conditions. A more imaginative public utility approach to banking needs to recognise that mis-selling is the nearly inevitable result of ambitious RoE targets. The starting point in reform has to be a new business model which combines two key features: first, much lower RoE targets of less than 10% plus, second, charging bank fees on some declared basis to recover the costs of current account and other basic services. Retail banking is a prime case for social licensing, probably on a regional basis, to take account of differences in regional property markets and business loan requirements and to include some basic rules about loan to value and such like to prevent property price bubbles. Any new experiment in social licensing could hardly produce worse results than the existing system of PLC chains whose outcomes are dysfunctional for private and business customers.

Notes to Chapter 4

1 Barclays' RoE of 7.8% in 2012 is the 'adjusted' return. This is different from the statutory RoE, also presented in the 2012 accounts because it excludes a number of items which, in this year, significantly reduce profit: these include provisions for fines (e.g. from libor fixing); customer redress (e.g from PPI mis-selling); and accounting adjustments (KPMG 2013). Barclays' statutory RoE in 2012 was -1.9%, compared with the 'adjusted' or core RoE of 7.8%. Looking across the business segments, the largest differences were in UK retail banking (3.1% vs 16%), Barclaycard (15.2% vs 22.1%) and in corporate banking (-3.7% vs 5.5%) (Barclays 2012). These provisions could be viewed as exceptional, not reflecting the underlying or core operating performance. However, they also reflect the business model of the banks where pressures to sell can lead to very expensive consequences.

2 Since 2009, overall financing advanced to SMEs has fallen almost 25% from £46bn to £34bn in 2012. The cost of financing has increased and SME risk profiles have been sharply revised upwards. Margins in SME lending have increased for both overdrafts and term loans by 2.0% and 1.5% respectively, while rejections have risen sharply from 4.2% to

15.3% for overdrafts, and from 6.1% to 16.3% for term loans, reflecting adjustments in SME risk rating – above average risk rated SMEs now represent 28% (9% in 2008) and low risk firms dropped to 19% (42% in 2008). According to Bank of England data, for the three months to August 2013, bank lending to both SMEs and large businesses continues to fall (Bank of England 2013); indeed, repayments have exceeded new loans so that net lending to SMEs has fallen. Even though interest rates have been low, these have not been reflected in the cost of borrowing which, for smaller SMEs, has increased by 20% since bottoming out in May 2009, with spreads over the base rate considerably higher than pre-crisis.

Chapter 5

Changing the frame:
there's more than one show in town

Like it or not, the free market economy is the only show in town. Britain is competing in an increasingly impatient and globalised economy, in which the competition is getting ever stiffer.
Boris Johnson, Margaret Thatcher Lecture (2013).

There were not one but several economies.
Fernand Braudel, *The Structures of Everyday Life* (1981).

Introduction

The case studies in this book point to the problem. Business models work in particular ways, and in crucial areas these are failing the national economy. But the problem is not confined to the corporate world; there is also a crucial failure in government policy. This means that we are confronted with a double and therefore intractable problem. It will be necessary to shift public policy before or alongside any change in corporate behaviour. And this is the issue that we explore in this final chapter. This means that we do not end the book with a list of policy fixes for telecoms, retail banking or the dairy industry. Instead we ask questions about the framework for government policy and corporate action. How, we ask, might this be changed?; what are the alternatives?; and how might industrial and economic policy be reframed to secure prosperity?[1]

Look at the quotations at the top of this page. Taken together, the words of London's Conservative mayor, Boris Johnson, and the late French *Annales School* historian Fernand Braudel suggest both the difficulty of and the potential for change. Since 1979 corporate business, London finance, the major parties and the Treasury have all operated with a particular concept of '*the* economy'. Here economic life is understood as a single reality that poses a single set of problems that can be tackled with generic solutions. Boris Johnson's words exemplify this singular framing: 'the free market economy is the only show in town.' And since this economy is now globalised, the imperative is to make 'the market' work better for national competitiveness in 'the global race'. Successful competition will deliver beneficial results for individuals, firms and nations alike. In this world there is no alternative framework.

Compare and contrast this with the words of Fernand Braudel, who takes a different view and recognises multiple economies. Before Braudel, economic historians of the early modern period had focussed on the economy of the market. They argued that this was the dynamic medium of commerce and innovation that would in due course deliver industrial revolution, Western imperialism and much else. Against this, in his *Civilization and Capitalism* volumes Braudel argued that from the 15th to the 18th century there were two further economic zones, one above and one below the market. Most of the world's population lived in a quite different, mundane and slow-moving *infra economy* of 'material life'. This was organised around immediate production and consumption rather than exchange. At the same time, above the market was a *supra economy* of a few insiders. In the early modern period these initiates engaged in long distance trade and speculation as they managed exchange under the aegis of the state (1981, p. 23).[2] Braudel's three-level scheme is specific to the early modern period, but his strategy of recognising multiplicity applies just as well to the present day. As a corrective to the Boris Johnson-like framing, we therefore follow Braudel by arguing the need to explore present day economic life in ways that recognise its multiplicity.

The three case studies are important. This is because they help us to open up ways of resisting generic understandings and thinking, instead, about the specificities of different sectoral economies.[3] But as noted above, it is not enough to focus on public policy, business models and their unintended consequences within each sector. If we are to displace government policies that treat the economy as an abstract single reality, or to challenge generic corporate business models with their commitment to shareholder value, we need to relate sector specifics to a larger economic and political argument. Here again Braudel shows the way.

- First, without mechanically transposing his three-layer descriptive scheme, we can draw on his idea of several distinct zones or spheres of economic life. The idea of an infra economy can be rethought in the context of current British specifics. To do this we reframe 'the economy' by talking about a zone of activity which

we call the *foundational economy*. This is an infra economy producing mundane goods and services which is beneath notice for
much of the time.

- Second, we can take Braudel's brilliant contrarian insight that
  capitalism is not only about the establishment of a free competitive market but also about entrenching an anti-market (contre
  marché) system in which the state is the guarantor of a monopoly
  that benefits a few. Again, the nature and form of state intervention and the forms of monopoly need to be rethought for our
  times. To do this we reframe politics by returning to the idea of
  government as experiment that we explored in the introduction,
  and add a paradoxical corollary. We suggest that the British government since 1979 has not only been stuck in a single framing
  of competition and markets, but has also been incapable of recognising that in many sectors government guarantees profitable
  monopolies for corporates.

With this work of reorientation it is possible to rethink policy
intervention. We start from a critique of current corporate practice
and government policy, and argue that a 'point value' logic lies
at the heart of the mismanagement of the foundational. Then we
suggest that the post-1979 policy experiment is now using 'bolt-
ons', like industrial policy, to ensure that state policy answers
exigencies without addressing fundamentals. But if we follow
Braudel to think about the foundational economy and the character of state-sustained corporate monopolies it is possible to reframe
policy and imagine new kinds of intervention. No doubt there are
many possibilities, but we have a specific proposal. We argue that
foundational firms or sectors drawing on household expenditure
or tax revenue within a catchment area *should be placed under
an explicit obligation to meet specified economic and social objectives*. We argue, that is, for experiments with *social licensing*. Then
we move on to suggest that if we want to learn well then social
licensing experiments will be better carried out in diverse ways in
different places. But this has a directly political corollary because
British government is so centralised that at present this is not possible. The implication is that economic singularity and political
centralisation will have to be tackled together if the negotiation
of appropriate social licenses reflecting different local and regional
agendas is to be achieved. One size cannot fit all either politically
or industrially.

The foundational economy

Everyday life consists of the little things one hardly notices in space and time.
(Braudel 1981, p. 29).

How to make another economy visible and engage everyday life in its economic and social specificities? As we have just noted, we do this by drawing on our case studies and connecting these with national and international specifics. The three cases in this book are chosen because they deal with network or branch activities that are substantially sheltered from local and global competition. But with the relative failure of British manufacturing such activities have become increasingly important in the British economy. In the face of global competition the manufacturing sector which employed seven million at the beginning of the 1970s now employs just over two million and accounts for no more than 11% of GDP. At the same time, as in other high income countries over the last forty years, employment in the UK in health, education and welfare has substantially increased (Buchanan *et al.* 2013). All in all, what we are calling the foundational economy has become far more important.

So what is the foundational economy? We define this as the economic zone that produces mostly mundane and sometimes taken-for-granted goods and services that have three inter-related characteristics: first, they are *necessary to everyday life*; second, they are consumed by *all citizens* regardless of income; and third, they are therefore *distributed according to population through branches and networks*. The list of such activities includes: the privatised pipe and cable utilities together with transport; some traditionally private activities such as retail banking, supermarket food retailing and food processing; and some traditionally state-provided activities including health, education, and welfare or social care, which are now increasingly outsourced.

There are resonances here with Braudel's 'material life', but since much has changed since the eighteenth century, the specificities are also very different. The pipe and cable utilities have much the same sustaining significance for urban twenty-first century Britain as food supply in the early modern world; while energy prices are now a source of grievance, much as high grain prices were in the eighteenth century. In less fortunate countries, natural, economic and political disasters, such as earthquakes, hyper-inflation or state failure are defined by the complete breakdown of the foundational economy. Meanwhile, many foundational services in the UK are not barely noticed 'little things' but big issues; the quality of health, education and care is endlessly publicly debated and the provision of social security or childcare is a matter of political controversy. Although healthcare and public schooling are free at the point of use in the UK, the foundational is also increasingly entangled with market exchanges, not least by the outsourcing of state-funded activities to private contractors. More broadly, the foundational now has post-industrial strategic importance because the cost, quality and security of foundational services or products such as energy costs and medical care are generally more important for welfare than the purchase price of tradable goods such as tablet computers and cars (which in any case depend on foundationally-created infrastructures).

If we shift from consumption to production it quickly becomes clear that the foundational economy is very large. The obvious and immediate corollary is that how it is managed and developed is similarly important. The relevant evidence on employment in the UK is summarised in exhibit 5.1

The figures show that one third of the UK's workforce is employed in the foundational economy with nearly 10% in private and privatised activities and twice that number in state-provided and

		England		Wales	
		Employees No.	Share of total employment %	Employees No.	Share of total employment %
Private, state and state-supported foundational economy activities	Private sector activities	2,256,674	9.4	122,772	9.8
	State and state-supported activities	5,744,372	23.8	353,247	28.1
	Total foundational economy activities	8,001,046	33.2	476,019	37.8
Comparators	Total employees	24,104,050		1,259,038	
	Manu-facturing	2,066,567	8.6	129,680	10.3

Exhibit 5.1 Private sector, state and state-supported employment in foundational economy activities

Source: Nomis

state-funded activities. The number working in capital-intensive pipe and cable utilities is small, but retailing remains labour intensive with some 440,000 employed in retail banking, 1 million in supermarkets and some 323,000 in food processing. But by far the largest number of foundational workers are to be found in the state or para-state sectors of health, education and welfare/social care which in total employ 4.6 million. In the UK, such services (which have in the past been delivered locally by the state) are now increasingly delivered by the para-state (including private sector firms, charities and social enterprises), where some or all of the funding comes from government. The number employed in the para-state sector has already grown to one third of those directly employed by the state.

The foundational economy is partly financed indirectly by tax revenues and partly by direct household expenditure. The latter is easily tracked. Data on household expenditure shows how foundational activity reaches into every household in the country in a way that tells us that such activities are both geographically distributed and in some measure sheltered from global competition.

Exhibit 5.2 shows that in 2011 £141 or nearly 30% of all household expenditure went on foundational activities with the big ticket items being £55 on groceries (excluding alcoholic drink), £42 on pipe and cable utilities and £34 mainly on car fuel. The other notable point is that, though expenditure on these objects varies with income, *all households are foundational consumers*. So, for instance, food and non-alcoholic drink accounts for 15.9% of total expenditure in the poorest Q1 households and 9% in the richest Q5 households. The implication, as we noted above, is that foundational activities are both distributed and sheltered: they are *distributed* across the UK because schooling or retailing follow populations; and they are *sheltered* either because they are – implicitly or explicitly politically – franchised by the state, or because they are protected from direct, non-territorial competition.

All economic classifications, including measures like GDP, are constructs and the notion of foundational economy is no exception. It is neither a 'natural' nor a privileged 'scientific' measure. Like 'manufacturing' it is a bracketing category or tool that may do useful economic and political work (Mitchell 2002, 2008). What such bracketing devices include and exclude is necessarily somewhat arbitrary, and economic activities can always be measured in other ways. However what is important is what they make visible and the work that they do. This field of visibility can be developed in different ways. For example, for Sen (1985) and Nussbaum (2000) the

	Quintile group					
	Q1	Q2	Q3	Q4	Q5	All/ average
Persons per household	1.4	2.1	2.4	2.8	3.1	2.4
TOTAL EXPENDITURE	£198.20	£323.85	£444.65	£573.60	£878.35	£483.60
Food and non-alcoholic drink	£31.60	£44.95	£54.80	£63.50	£79.10	£54.70
Percentage share of total expenditure	15.9%	13.9%	12.3%	11.1%	9.0%	11.3%
Expenditure per person in household	£22.57	£21.40	£22.83	£23.09	£25.93	£22.79
Electricity, gas, other fuels and water	£18.20	£24.85	£29.50	£34.05	£42.10	£29.80
Percentage share of total expenditure	9.2%	7.7%	6.6%	5.9%	4.8%	6.2%
Expenditure per person in household	£13.00	£11.83	£12.29	£12.38	£13.80	£12.42
Telephony, internet and postal services	£6.85	£10.00	£12.60	£15.15	£19.00	£12.70
Percentage share of total expenditure	3.5%	3.1%	2.8%	2.6%	2.2%	2.6%
Expenditure per person in household	£4.89	£4.76	£5.25	£5.51	£6.23	£5.29
Rail, bus and other fares (excluding cars)	£3.60	£5.60	£8.20	£12.30	£21.50	£10.10
Percentage share of total expenditure	1.8%	1.7%	1.8%	2.1%	2.4%	2.1%
Expenditure per person in household	£2.57	£2.67	£3.42	£4.47	£7.05	£4.21
Car spares, patrol, diesel and repairs and servicing	£8.50	£20.00	£31.05	£44.85	£65.95	£34.10
Percentage share of total expenditure	4.3%	6.2%	7.0%	7.8%	7.5%	7.1%
Expenditure per person in household	£6.07	£9.52	£12.94	£16.31	£21.62	£14.21
Spending on foundational economy activities	£68.75	£105.40	£136.15	£169.85	£227.65	£141.40
Percentage share of total expenditure	34.7%	32.5%	30.6%	29.6%	25.9%	29.2%
Expenditure per person in household	£49.11	£50.19	£56.73	£61.76	£74.64	£58.92

Exhibit 5.2 Weekly family expenditure by UK households on selected foundational economy goods and services in 2011

Note: UK households are arranged by quintile group as measured by income: Q1 are the poorest fifth and Q5 are the richest fifth

Source: Family Spending, ONS

concept of human capability highlights how people need the support of a well-functioning foundational economy if they are to flourish and develop their capabilities. However the foundational is almost invisible to British policy makers both because economic activity is not classified in this way, and because they prefer to work with the abstractions of competition and markets which assume that what is appropriate to globally competitive industries is similarly appropriate to sheltered parts of the economy.

The rationale for the category of the foundational is therefore as much political as economic. This is partly because the category highlights a part of the economy that is both important and neglected. It is also because it throws into relief the uneasy political relations between the state and the corporate controllers of the private and privatised distribution of everything foundational from electricity to groceries. So, for instance, many parts of the foundational economy are defined by a triangular relation between three dominant players (state, privatised utilities and supermarkets). This means that the political game of the utilities and supermarkets is to forestall or deflect the exercise of state policies that might reduce their profitability and, more positively, to secure what amounts to state patronage. The state is always potentially sovereign, both because it is the major funder of outsourced activities and because it regulates many privatised and private forms of economy activity which therefore operate in a politically constructed context of profitability. This political construction of profit is most obvious for the utilities where regulators control prices and set targets for acceptable return on assets, but it is also important in the private sector where, for instance, planning regulations give superstores effective territorial franchises.

Politically this tells us that 'neo-liberal' rhetoric about shrinking the state misses the point. The essential corporate project in the foundational zone is rather to manage the exercise of state power, and render the latter more amenable to influence. The implication is that this corporate effort needs to be counter-balanced by politically-negotiated social licensing of foundational firms and sectors. The state needs to be brought back in to exercise its powers differently. Meanwhile, our three case studies show how major corporations have successfully protected their option on profits, while in sectors such as rail and energy they have succeeded in passing the costs and risks of investment to the state. Often they have managed the state with trade narratives about the benefits delivered by private firms, which have made them (together with London finance) the dominant lobby in politics.[4] But tactics vary from sector to sector. As we have seen, in supermarkets the stereotyped business model has escaped challenge because firms do compete, deliver shareholder value and offer low prices (while the state remains incurious about the consequences for suppliers and supply chains). In retail banking the tactic has been to procrastinate about misconduct before paying fines for mis-selling and ostentatiously moving on without changing business models. But what lies at the core of these business models? We touched on the answer above – a commitment to point value – and it is to this that we now turn.

Point value

As applied to stocks, the underlying idea is simple enough. The investment value of a stock is the present value of all future dividends. If we can fairly estimate these and select a suitable discount rate, the calculation of present value becomes merely a problem in higher algebra.
Benjamin Graham (1939) reviewing the first edition of John Burr Williams (1938) *The Theory of Investment Value.*

This was how readers of the *Journal of Political Economy* in 1939 learnt about a new method of valuation, developed by a Harvard PhD student. This was to colonise the capitalist world in the next fifty years and displace older accounting practices and the economic assumptions of authors like Frank Knight (1921) and J.M. Keynes (1936) about how uncertainty and the incalculable limited the role of financial calculation. The techniques now taught as discounted cash flow offer a way of converting any future stream of payments over time into a 'point value' in the present. As Graham notes, the future is converted into the present through algebra which requires only the inputs of estimated cash flows and an appropriate discount rate. The time value of money formulae were originally proposed by Burr Wilson for portfolio investment decisions and subsequently extended to physical investment project appraisal. And the underlying point value assumption (though divested of the algebra) has since become the active principle for mismanaging the foundational economy.

The consequence is that our form of financialised and globalised capitalism is historically distinctive because it no longer sees value as a stream of benefits over time divided between stakeholders holding established claims within a given territory with taken–for-granted boundaries. Instead, encouraged by formulae about discounting and the time value of money, and normalised by the institutions of shareholder value, the tendency has increasingly been to privilege low costs or high profits in individual transactions at a node, whilst marginalising economic or social consequences elsewhere in the chain of production and consumption. This is the core logic of *point value* (Bowman *et al*. 2012b). The longer term is ignored because distant benefits and costs have low monetary value with discount rates of 5% or more.[5] At the same time local, regional and national stakeholders have no legitimate claims over the character of transactions because global chains are justified whenever they increase profits or reduce prices (classically by tapping low wages in developing countries).

The commitment to point value has been set in motion over the last twenty years in a particular management accounting framework and conjunctural context which has imposed contradictory financial demands via capital and product markets. On the one hand the capital market demands shareholder value and sets sectoral rate requirements for return on equity and earnings growth in a frame where all firms are expected to earn abnormal profits. On the other hand, state authorities and globalisation have enforced forms of product market competition which ostensibly require low prices and modest margins. Since 2008 public sector point value pressures have further intensified with budget cuts, and social responsibility has increasingly been undermined by the brief to deliver value for money. The results have been self-defeating for the public sector, and have led to easy choices for the private sector.

- In the public sector, point value represents a narrow management accounting rationality. Because, while the state saves directly on wages and conditions in its provision of services, it picks up the tab elsewhere in the form of low wage dependence via housing benefit, health care costs and pensions. On the ground, in an activity such as adult care, the result may be twenty minute home visits, unpaid travel and wages effectively below the legal minimum for untrained care workers whose life time costs of subvention are considerable.
- In the private sector, point value boosts shareholder value in sheltered and in predatory corporations which pass problems on to others in the supply chain by shaving their margins. Indeed supplier margins may be captured, as Apple has done to its assembler Foxconn (Froud *et al*. 2014), or the major supermarkets have typically done to food processors in the meat or dairy sectors. The consequences in the British food supply chain have been low wages, low processing margins, broken national supply chains, and increases in imports (Bowman *et al*. 2012a).

Point value thus frames calculations of advantage in a way that disconnects them from broader social or economic concerns. Such calculations are enforced by trader mentalities and by predatory commitment to contracts. They flourish in the absence of incentives to think about supply chains and social linkages as enduring relations to be grown and developed. Any focus on long term social and economic benefits across sectors or on possible local socio-political obligations is pushed to the margins. Point value is justified, especially in the private sector, by the economic alibi that there is one best way to least cost – and this is point value. Furthermore, such arguments are often plausible because they can only be contradicted by those with substantial knowledge of sectoral specifics. But if we attend to those sectoral specifics we quickly find that there are very often better ways of trading.

For instance, our research into meat supply in the British supermarket chains suggests that point value arguments are misleading, even though those who practise them typically argue that there is no satisfactory alternative (Bowman *et al.* 2012a, pp. 47–57). Thus, three of the four major chains are buyer-led and make a large part of their profits by exercising trading power against producers and processors. However, the fourth UK supermarket chain, Morrisons, has a vertically-integrated meat supply chain with its own abattoir and processing plants. This runs more profitably and efficiently than those of the external suppliers used by the other chains. The reason for this is that Morrisons' own plants do not need to meet ever-changing orders. Instead, they are fully loaded with steady throughput. This means that they utilise labour effectively so that Morrisons' labour share of value added in processing is a very low 35%. Indeed, Morrisons uses the cash generated from meat processing to cross-subsidise a weak retail chain. The three other supermarket chains cannot do this because they have no manufacturing competence and must rely on buyer power. The lesson is clear: if you have the expertise of Morrisons to run an effective integrated supply chain the results pay just as well as point value trading.

It is clear that vertical disintegration and least cost outsourcing can close-off viable alternatives and damage supply chains by passing on costs elsewhere in the chain. However, it is embedded in the business models of dominant private and public sector business players. As long as business models deliver on narrow point value criteria, they will usually escape scrutiny (or find ways of managing criticism); this is certainly the case in supermarkets which have their alibi in the form of shareholder profits and low prices for consumers. And the dominance of point value thinking within government is indicated by the shareholder value objective of UK Financial Investments (UKFI), the agency which holds state shares in Britain's post-2008 bailed-out banks. Thus Lloyds is being encouraged to increase return on equity (RoE) towards 15% and achieve profitability so that it can be sold off, even though successive reports and inquiries regret the mis-selling of PPI by Lloyds and others. However UKFI does not identify mis-selling as the nearly inevitable consequence of a shareholder value target. It does not see that in the absence of the kind of supply chain available to the supermarkets to be squeezed, the only possible source of increased profits is customers. More generally, this kind of contradiction is generally invisible in Whitehall and Westminster because the objective of policy makers is not to challenge business models for cost recovery or question shareholder value targets. Instead the state sets as its task the promotion of market competition and the creation of a generically-supportive environment for established firms and inward investors through structural reform and horizontal measures that involve liberalising planning, deregulating employment law and lowering taxes.

The state as guarantor of monopoly

Most liberals and most Marxists have argued that capitalism involved above all the establishment of a free, competitive market. Braudel saw capitalism instead as the system of the antimarket (contre marché) … Here the role of the state was to contain the forces of the antimarket. For private markets did not arise merely to promote efficiency but also to 'eliminate competition'. But the state was a guarantor as well, a guarantor of monopoly- indeed its creator.
(Wallerstein 1991).

The quotation above presents Immanuel Wallerstein's reading of Braudel's history as an explicit theory, which Braudel himself did not do. Wallerstein did this by drawing out the assumptions implicit in the three volumes of *Civilization and Capitalism*. The contrast with other theorists of capitalism is instructive. The latter write (in liberal or critical variants) of the rise or imposition of the market and competition, but Braudel tells a different story. There was, he says, a separate 'capitalist game' (1982, p. 456); an anti-market zone of monopolisation and power that manipulated exchanges to secure advantage. There were 'certain groups of privileged actors… engaged in circuits and calculations that ordinary people knew nothing of'

(1981, p. 24). The state might then be the creator or guarantor of monopoly by 'privileged companies' in this zone, as well as the promoter of competition in the market place (1982, pp. 413, 421). In a suitably modified form Braudel's insight is equally relevant to present day circumstances.

To see this we need first to return to our earlier argument about the British state. This, we suggested, is locked in a cycle in which it is continually repeating a failed experiment. Trapped in an imaginary about competition and markets, the result is that we have a non-learning state. If we draw on STS thinking about the character of experiment and learning our argument looks like this:

- government is about *experimenting*;
- experimenting is about *learning*;
- learning is about *building on successes but also about making mistakes*; and
- learning is also about *recognising these as mistakes, and moving on*.

Moreover, it is helpful to distinguish between four different kinds of learning:

1. learning *within the framework*, which uses the latter to judge between outcomes;
2. learning by *adapting the framework*, in order to remedy a detectable problem;
3. learning as *gaming the framework* in order to turn it to advantage (for instance by complying formally with performance metrics); and finally there is
4. learning as *large scale reframing* during which the validity of the whole framework is undermined.

All these forms of learning are appropriate in different circumstances. However, our interest is in the last of these options, and in particular in the circumstances in which it becomes impossible. So using this simple framework, our argument is that key parts of the British state – and in particular the Treasury – have lost the capacity to think about reframing because they have become dogmatically committed to a single form of experiment within one unquestioned framework: 'TINA' ('there is no alternative') was Margaret Thatcher's slogan. Two or three decades on this has become 'TINAF' ('there is no alternative framework'). This is the working assumption of New Labour and Coalition ministries. In the face of failure they accept that things are not necessarily working very well, but they favour learning *within* the framework (learning mode 1), or by *adapting* it in small ways (learning mode 2). While private operators display increasing skill at gaming the system (learning mode 3), government is unable to question the overall framework, and continues to try to impose an abstract version of competition and market rather than exploring alternatives. The fourth mode of learning has become impossible. If this seems an exaggeration, consider the official determination to persist with rail franchising in the completely dysfunctional railway financing system (Bowman *et al.* 2013b).

These ideas are expressed in STS language but are also entirely consonant with current political science understanding. As Moran (2007) has argued, we have created a hyper-active state where government is endlessly accumulating evidence of failure and constantly promising to do better with new reforms which often involve changing the machinery of government. There is no end to the Select Committee reports and commissions of inquiry. But our argument is not that the state is incapable of learning. Rather it is that what it can learn is strictly limited because failures are never attributed to the framework, and the basic assumptions about competition and market are never called into question. These confusions are not confined to government. They are echoed in much writing in mainstream economics and political science. To take a single example, King and Crewe (2013) in *The Blunders of our Government* analyse policy fiascos (including the poll tax and public private partnerships on the London Underground). However, since they work on the assumption that privatisation is 'now almost universally accepted as having been a success' (p. 5), assumptions about the virtue of markets remain unchallenged.

As broadsheet newspaper readers can see most mornings, the result is that the state is in a perpetual state of contrition about its failings yet constantly repeating old blunders and stumbling into new fiascos. The 2012 debacle about the allocation of the West Coast main line franchise did not lead to any focus on the issue of how both of the corporate finalists in the bidding had made highly optimistic assumptions about sustained economic growth and passenger numbers; instead Department of Transport civil servants did penance for their failure to calculate risk premiums correctly. The West Coast bidders had covered their optimism about revenue in a now traditional way by offering the state most of their premium payments in later years so that they had an option to walk away without large penalties in mid franchise after profit making in the early years (Bowman *et al.* 2013a). If the corporate bidders were not offered this 'get out' they would of course be very reluctant to bid. So the institutionalisation of this non-learning, and repeated attempts to impose the competition and markets framework continues.

So what might an alternative look like after this thirty-year experiment? On the evidence of our three cases, outcomes are perverse because repeated attempts to impose the doxic frame do not result in a movement towards competition. Instead, they install the state as the unwitting sponsor of the kind of monopoly identified by Braudel and exemplified in the early modern period by a trading company like the East India Company. Again, this perverse and unrecognised outcome is a consequence of the limits of the framework. Public policy through the 30 year experiment has ostentatiously enforced and encouraged competition which is technically defined in a narrow mainstream economic sense. This means that public policy is about policing market share, controlling mergers between established players and encouraging new entrants. At the same time, however, this does nothing to prevent monopoly in the sense defined by Braudel: that is by the exercise of power by corporate players to set rules of the game which maintain generous profit margins at a cost to others; and to do so by lobbying the state, just like early modern trading companies. In our three cases, the rules of the game are incorporated in (politically unchallenged and unrecognised) firm and sector business models. These deliver the local requirement for shareholder value and focus the efforts of all the major corporates on point value trading transactions. Social needs such as telecoms investment, or the disadvantages of squeezing other stakeholders (such as the suppliers to supermarkets or the customers in banking) are ignored. And though we have focussed on just three industries, we suggest that these stories could be matched with others from social provision: the costly marketisation of the NHS may well impede cooperative health care provision, and, community care outsourcing combines poor quality of care with low pay and inferior conditions for carers.

Crucially, this is a missed opportunity. This is because across large parts of the foundational economy the state already has, or could find, the levers it needs to require corporate players to make alternative calculations that would work to the advantage of communities, sustainability or supply chains. But the opportunity is being missed because, as we have seen, the state cannot see beyond the single and abstract point-value understanding of economic outcomes that it shares with mainstream economics and the corporate players. State policies devised in this frame cannot attend to the *specificities* of forms of competition in product and capital markets. The state lacks basic conceptual tools to think differently. At the same time the state has close relations with powerful private sector clients, and its capacity to think independently of those clients has become limited. This inability has been further exacerbated by the substantial failure of independent thinkers to offer alternative forms of economic framing. Finally, the failure has been catastrophically aggravated by the centralisation of the British state combined with policy bolt-ons that create an illusion of progress.

Policy change: the antidote fallacy and bolt-ons

'(Privatisation) was one of the central means of reversing the corrosive and corrupting effects of socialism. Just as nationalisation was at the heart of the collectivist programme by which Labour governments sought to remodel British society, so privatisation is at the centre of any programme of re-claiming territory for freedom.'
Margaret Thatcher, quoted in David Parker (2009, p. 528).

If the primary problem has been the fixity of the framework, matters have been greatly complicated, and confusions been increased, by the kinds of policy variation encouraged by the culture and habits of thought of the British political classes. The opening quotation from Margaret Thatcher illustrates the part of this cultural problem that was crucially important in the early programmatic stages of the post-1979 experiment. Thatcher thought in terms of Manichean oppositions between capitalist good and socialist evil. It was time to overthrow the policies of post-war socialism and she thought in terms of the antidote fallacy. Radical reform could only be secured by reversing the policies of her predecessors on the basis of generic assumptions about the state and the market, public and private. She thus inverted the values supposedly attached to these terms by her enemies. Hence, privatisation – the antidote to nationalisation – was constructed around the idea that one form of ownership is intrinsically superior to the other and would deliver the future.

Thatcher's antidote fallacy should be dead. It invokes a crude cartoon of British history which works by opposing state and market in ways that are irrelevant and unhelpful when the contract state now ensures state and market are interpenetrated; and it then adds a very curious supposition that, if generic ownership policy (a) fails, the opposite policy (b) must succeed (without recognising that specifics will complicate both). But antidote still resonates in the media and in popular opinion which is currently angered by manifestly failed privatisations like rail or energy and suspicious about the rest. It is encouraged by a blindly adversarial party system and a tabloid-driven culture of public debate by scapegoating where change would involve 'throwing the scoundrels out'. Against this background, it is hardly surprising that British opinion polls now suggest broad based majority support for a return to public ownership in many privatised sectors. The results of a YouGov poll in November 2013 were revealing.

> *The majority of the British public – including the majority of Conservative voters – support nationalising the energy and rail companies. 68% of the public say the energy companies should be run in the public sector, while only 21% say they should remain in private hands. 66% support nationalising the railway companies while 23% think they should be run privately. The British people also tend strongly to prefer a publicly-run National Health Service (as it is now) and a publicly-run Royal Mail (as it was until this year).*
> (YouGov 2013).

But such positions have little traction in Whitehall and Westminster. Partly, this is because the inversion of the inversion (antidote fallacy squared) is more a cry of pain from the electorate than a worked out policy proposal. And partly because reframing is more than usually disruptive when government lacks the sectoral expertise to think differently, given four key political and administrative features of the Whitehall and Westminster machine.

1. In many parts of Whitehall, original thought which puts the competition *framework* into question is career-threatening and therefore dangerous for civil servants. The think tanks on the Westminster campus around College Green have since before 1979 been in the business of providing front bench-ready policies developed by researchers who often aspire to cross the Green into the House. For those with ideas, it is better form to *join in* the conversation rather than seek to disrupt it.
2. Executive competence is proved by implementing some part of a group project (an example would be the reform of the school system) whose aims and coordinates are doxic for the whole political class. A kind of innovative conformity is rewarded with trust and promotion in the administrative machine; much of the political conflict and dissent is then organised around personal

factions and followings (Brownites vs Blairites) where the prize is executive office and policy differences are few.

3. By the 2010s, departments such as the Department for Environment, Food and Rural Affairs (DEFRA) or the Department for Business, Innovation and Skills (BIS) have very little remaining sectoral expertise as a basis for challenging the commitment to point value versions of markets and trading, This is the result of Treasury control of the spending departments and the commitment to generic competition and markets in all the economic ministries whose notion of intervention is now limited to market failure.

4. As a further part of this, the Treasury's intelligence is limited by its reliance on young graduates who quickly leave for higher salaries in the private sector precisely because they have generic economic skills rather than expertise in specific sectors of the economy (HM Treasury 2012). Those who stay and progress rapidly upwards have thoroughly conventional minds. And so the Treasury, like the Lex column on the back page of the *Financial Times*, represents the reincarnation of British amateurism, which allows quick and confident judgement of a technical brief.

If reframing is unlikely under these conditions, policies have to be varied in the light of previous disappointments, unexpected events and undeniable problems. As a result British policy makers have adapted to change by holding on to generic simplifications which simplify matters in ways that everybody can understand, and then by *bolting on* auxiliary policies (most recently in the form of industrial policy).

So, for instance, the 2008 finance-led crisis revealed an 'unbalanced economy', inaugurated government-led austerity, and also had the potential to raise difficult questions about what pro-market and competition policies had achieved. However, despite the questions, BIS and others in central government have held on to the competition and markets frame together with the established policies of structural reform and labour flexibility. Alongside this they have bolted-on a more active industrial policy. This has been a sectorally-focused programme intended to remedy national performance deficiencies (see Bentham *et al.* (2013)). Favoured sectors for targeted intervention have included advanced manufacturing, automotive, pharmaceuticals and life sciences, digital media and green technology (see David Willets' 'eight great technologies' (2013)). Sectors have typically been technology-intensive, producing tradable and exportable goods and services with potential for enhancing national competitiveness, for instance with the help of 'catapult centres' where state money is used to underpin commercialisation of innovation in high value manufacturing. The fit between the basic frame and the bolt-ons has been helped by the fact that academics such as Mazzucato (2013) have been independently arguing for selective state intervention on the grounds of market failure in early stage innovation.

But is this going to work? The answer is that this seems unlikely. With the UK factory sector in foreign ownership, trade performance is dismal because ambitions are limited and there is high demand for imported components, which account for 45% of the purchases in each motor car. In addition, the focus on advanced technology is likely to give very little leverage on output growth, productivity or trade performance. The advanced technological sectors form a very small part of the British economy. In the UK, the research and development intensive sectors account for 1.76% of GDP and much of manufacturing employment is in mundane sectors like food manufacture. Thus, the latter together with food production employs twice as many as in all the favoured manufacturing sectors combined. More fundamentally, Gordon (2012) has analysed historical growth trajectories and repeatedly questioned whether digital technologies are as transformative in the present day as were universal electrification and the internal combustion engine in an earlier era. The cautious response would be that transformation requires a top-to-bottom reformatting of the economy which is the work of more than a generation and limits early pay offs.

'Bolt-ons' like industrial policy may have an important role to play in the political management of a restive electorate because they allow the political and policy making classes to perform the idea that they have learnt from experience and are responding to changed circumstances with new policies. However, they are a poor substitute for more fundamental thinking and learning about our economies.

Social license

> I here suggest that big business, in the American system, exists and derives its right to exist under, and only under, a tacit social contract. This social contract requires management of big business to assume certain responsibilities. Assumption and fulfillment of them entitles big business to the privileges it receives from the State, and to acquiescence in their existence by the economic community they affect and serve.
> (Berle 1962).

An alternative vision is possible. As we noted in Chapter 1, this book revives an earlier tradition of liberal collectivism whose high point was in the 1930s, the last period when the economy faced a crisis of the magnitude of that which followed the 2008 crash. If English liberal collectivists such as John Maynard Keynes led in technical economic thought, their American counterparts such as Adolf Berle made the political argument in a country where Roosevelt's New Deal had encouraged progressive political thinking.[6] It is ironic that Berle is now narrowly remembered as the author of the distinction between ownership and control, because the argument of his classic 1932 book was for 'the assertion of community interests' against those of both owners and managers (Ertürk *et al*. 2008, pp. 45–53). Our quote above shows that he never relinquished this view and was arguing in the 1960s that corporate big business exists under a tacit 'social contract' where its right to operate is balanced by social obligation and requires the consent of the 'economic community' that it serves.

Within this alternative liberal collectivist tradition the task has always been 'the assertion of community interests' through formal politics. But what does this mean? How to curb the commitment to point value that frames so much foundational economic activity in the public and the private sectors? How to reform firm and sector business models that have irresponsibility to others built into them? And how to find a policy lever which can engage local specifics in a range of firms and sectors in ways that challenge the competition and markets framework, without lapsing into another generic frame which promises more than it delivers?

Berle's requirement might be met in various ways, for instance by some form of tripartite corporatism involving employers, organised labour and the state, in which they trade promises about macro variables like rates of wage increase and social expenditure. Such agreements can be a useful part of the tool kit of macro-economic management, but our search is for devices and ways of thinking that are more specific to localities, regions and sectors. This also means radical changes in the present system of corporate governance whose current ambition is limited to the rearrangement of the order and priority of stakeholder claims around individual firms. That will not suffice because our search is for approaches that are more responsive to civic concerns and use the power of the state to secure collective goods from firm and sector.

It is clear that there is need for an intellectual gestalt shift. New practices of intervention will depend on new languages with concepts and measures that offer alternative visions of the economic and social compact that ties firms and sectors to citizens under the aegis of the state within a definite area (whether local or regional as much as national). It will require a political justification framed in a new language about the *obligations of firms and sectors* that connects with a much broader (and less technically GDP-centred) concept of innovation than that promoted by mainstream economists. This is because firms and sectors will need to change to secure long term sustainability and resilience within a foundational economy capable of delivering high quality and accessible economic and social services. This in turn will require economic justifications which frame and press for diverse measures of *chain value* against the logic of *point value*, and so challenge current private and public sector business models. One way forward is to think in terms of, and to experiment with, *social licenses* in the context of the foundational economy.

The notion of 'social license' is most familiar in the mining industry, particularly in the developing world. Here it takes the form of a formal or informal agreement between an investor seeking to extract natural resources, and the community affected by these activities. It may cover labour conditions, environmental standards, the sharing of economic benefits and other locally important concerns such as the protection of sacred sites (Socialicense undated; miningfacts.org undated). Our suggestion is that something comparable to the more formal version of mining social license might be applied to firms and sectors in the foundational economy. Here we are working by analogy. The extractive industries seek immobile natural resources, but so too do private sector operators in the foundational economy which tap the household spend and taxes of an immobile population. In mining, as in the foundational economy, a limited number of operators are granted the right to extract. The fundamental rationale is the thus the same. In the foundational economy, as in countries sitting on large mineral deposits, businesses need to earn the right to extract cash from a territory rather than expect sweeteners to operate locally.

How might social licensing work in the foundational economy? Our suggestions which are tentative and for discussion are as follows:

- Licensing would be an explicit arrangement that gave contracting enterprises or sectors privileges and rights to trade whilst placing them under reciprocal obligations to *offer social returns*: a formal licensing system would make the right to trade dependant on providing a service that meets relevant criteria of community responsibility on issues such as sourcing, training or payment of living wages. As noted earlier, this is not just because being 'socially responsible' is a good in itself or burnishes corporate reputation, but also because these issues are important for promoting the sustainability of services – economic and social – of good quality and that are widely accessible over the longer term.

- The scale and scope of licensing agreements would vary. They might be with whole sectors, including all the firms above a certain size threshold. In other cases, where firm size and market position varied greatly within a sector, it might be more appropriate to have separate firm agreements. For example, the sourcing obligations on the big four supermarket chains would probably be different from those placed on smaller chain Waitrose, or the regional chain of Booths. Note, as a part of this, that the 'community' is not a natural domain but a variable political and economic unit, influenced for example by local and regional government forms and boundaries. Agreements, with rewards and sanctions such as variation in corporate tax rates, would clearly need to work round relevant national and EU legislation at the same time as putting the appropriateness of such rules into question.

The rationale for such agreements is socio-political. Foundational enterprises are in direct and mutually-dependent relations with communities or user-groups. As we have seen, they often benefit from limited competition and sheltered streams of revenue as they draw their customers and profits from communities in specific catchment areas. The argument is that in return for their sheltered existence they owe something to those communities or groups, and therefore should be brought within a new kind of regime. To reframe the foundational economy as a matter of social license is thus to insist that the foundational is not simply about point-value economic transactions, but also about reciprocal social relations within local, regional and national spaces. The provision of mundane goods and services in the foundational economy is intertwined with the multiple identities of people as consumers, workers, and local residents so that prices, wages and quality of life would need to be triangulated across politically negotiated spaces. The aim would be a new world of social licensing where it was no longer so easy for councils to collude with payment of below minimum wages, or for supermarkets to ignore local concerns about sourcing.

The proposal is thus for an extension of government which takes the burden of expectation from (corporate) governance as we presently understand it. It is an extension because foundational firms and sectors are already implicated in government. As we noted earlier, the foundational economy is more or less *state dependent* and rests on implicit or explicit political license. The state is not a Leviathan which strikes fear into the hearts of managements with its competition commissions. Instead, and like the states described by Braudel, it gives foundational enterprises and sectors a sheltered life – most typically by managing market competition in a territorial area. Privatisation, outsourcing and public private partnership is the early modern sale of the monopolies reworked for our time with the difference that the state now grants profitable concessions and gets little in return.[7] This state protection may be explicit and contractual, as with rail franchising or social care; or regulatory, as in the relation between supermarkets and planning permissions. Alternatively, the social license may involve not disturbing *de facto* territorial monopolies as with bank branches; or may even include state inducements to invest as with rural broadband rollout. It is not sensible to try and deal with these problems about the neglect of community interest through the present system of corporate governance, which is necessarily firm-centred and concerned with balancing the stakeholder interests of owners, managers and workers.

The proposal for social licensing is simultaneously mundane and quite far reaching. It is mundane because in large parts of the foundational economy this is already happening. The logic of social licensing of private providers from tax revenue is already in place in the para-state sector, where the state outsources its services (as with the railways, prisons and security services, education, and health and social care), though this is usually focused on service to the customer rather than broader issues like the payment of living wages. However, in other parts of the foundational economy where revenue comes from households (as with retail banking or the supermarkets) there is no social licensing. To be exact, there is very little social licensing when revenue is private, although a council may insist that a developer or supermarket builds a doctor's surgery or some roads in return for planning permission. To treat the branch of a supermarket chain as a social license would thus require new policy mechanisms and new political understandings of the character of economic activity.

Thus out-of-town supermarket branches are socially-licensed *de facto* because British planning regulations limit direct competition between superstores and effectively give the successful applicant a license to take money from households in the surrounding area. Planning regulation PPS 6 makes out-of-town centre development subject to a test of 'need' so that one or two successful applications to build stores effectively close the door to competitors which cannot subsequently obtain permission because the need has already been met (Friends of the Earth 2005). A social licence approach then asks: if a supermarket chain benefits in this way, should it not be also required to think about the effect of its practices on its supply chains? Should not supermarkets selling milk and meat be required by licence to align with British producers and processors (as Tesco already does with some dairy producers)? And should they not also be informally encouraged to develop vertically-integrated processing so that they also take responsibility for processing (as Morrisons already does with meat)?

These are straightforward proposals, in the tradition of liberal collectivism. But then the question is: can they be implemented? And if so, then how? If we are stuck in a state that cannot learn to think outside its policy frameworks, then how might it be possible to move forward?

Decentralisation and pluralism

[L]ocal government is not to be used or seen as a way of frustrating the outcome of general elections.
(Norman Tebbit 1991, p. 61).

Conservative governments after 1979 were ruthless centralisers which effectively ended city-wide UK government in 1986 by abolishing the Greater London Council and the six metropolitan councils in the other major conurbations. As the quote from Norman Tebbit suggests, a senior Thatcher minister could see local government only as an obstructive agency that might frustrate central government plans legitimated every four or five years by national elections. New Labour after 1997 talked about, but never delivered, regional government partly because it could not work out what an extra level of government might do. The result is that only the Celtic nations have devolved government. England remains highly centralised – and all the more so after the quango regional development agencies were abolished in 2010 by the Coalition which now relies on business-led Local Economic Partnerships and various associations of local authorities in the conurbations to do the work of the long dead metropolitan councils.

But alongside this centralisation, as we have seen, the Westminster state has exhausted itself and decimated British industry in the

pursuit of its abstract commitment to markets and point value transactions, while major corporates have pursued point value regardless
of social costs. So the question is pressing. *At this juncture*, how
can we lever change? There can be no single right answer, but in the
present context there is one obvious response. *The British state needs
to be decentralised.* This is because all the experiments cannot take
place in a single location and all the experiments cannot take place
within a single framework.

To be sure, the balance between centralisation and decentralisation
(and the meaning of each term) depends on time and place. So we have
repeatedly cited Scott (1999) on the limits of a governmentality of
legibility and simplification, and represented the 30 year experiment
since 1979 as one more centralised experiment with thin knowledge
and metrics of success. But at the same time, centralised big government has had its brilliant successes. Most obviously there was the
creation of the post-war social settlement in the UK which delivered
subsistence old age pensions, a comprehensive health service free
at point of use, a system of secondary and tertiary education and a
commitment to decent housing backed by utility networks. Whatever
the failures of Labour's economic management and the absences of
thought about nationalisation of basic industries, Nye Bevan was
right when he described the settlement as 'the most remarkable piece
of social reconstruction the world has ever seen' (1951). The key
point, however, is that this success came under specific conditions.
First, the post-1945 moment was a progressive conjuncture when
liberal collectivists such as Keynes and Beveridge were empowered
by wartime mobilisation and the pressures of powerful unions and
a mass Labour party which included leaders like Bevan and Bevin.
Second, in policy areas such as health, the NHS reform imposed a
national system and required minimum standards by sweeping away
a jumble of private provision and local initiative (which involved
levelling up to the standards of successful local experiments like the
Tredegar Workmens' Medical Aid Society (Morgan 2008)).

So there are moments for centralisation, but this is not the pattern
that we need for the UK in the 2010s when we are suffering from 30
years of dogmatic, centralised experiment without any governmental
reflection on the framework and its consequences. In this context
devolution is the more sensible proposition. Politically, Wales and
Scotland are still tied to Whitehall in important ways, and post-
devolution they have not conducted experiments in the foundational
economy. But, in principle, devolved governments and regions are
in a position to ask territorially-relevant questions precisely because

they are different industrially, historically, politically and culturally. Further political devolution – probably to several levels, as envisaged in Plaid Cymru plans for West Wales – would allow industrial experiments to take different local or regional forms and for government to explore different forms of social licencing. Such devolution is needed at this juncture, if we are to turn the state back into an experimental apparatus capable of learning from its failures rather than simply repeating them. So *a truly experimental form of social licensing will need powerful and substantially autonomous elected authorities.*

This is our first substantive recommendation, but it cannot stand alone. We also need to think hard about what counts as successful – and therefore about measures of success. The idea that there is one best way is currently deeply entrenched in the national policy making machine. Significantly, the discussion of 'industrial policy' in the UK is always of national policy with absolutely no discussion of regional geography and, at most, grudging recognition of sectoral differences outside the high-tech sector. This suggests that a 'one size fits all' assumption will also have to be abandoned if effective policy experiments are to be undertaken. A learning state will therefore also be one that cultivates a particular kind of *cognitive multiplicity* and *tolerance for difference*. What are taken to be important issues or good forms of policy in one location may not look that way in another, while what counts as success may look different from location to location. Thus, policies and *framings* for thinking about them and learning from them will also become pluralist. So this is our second substantive recommendation: *a truly experimental form of social licensing will cultivate forms of cognitive modesty* (Law and Williams 2014).

This, then, is our basic proposal. It is necessary to break out of the abstract market commitment to point value, and insofar as we have offered a new framework in the present paper, this is for a learning state in which there is both administrative devolution and cognitive multiplicity. But what might the social licensing of enterprises and sectors then mean in practice? The answer to this question will be locally or regionally variable. However a socially licensed enterprise or sector might be one that:

- *sustained itself economically*;
- offered fair value to *consumers*;
- was locally owned, or returned a percentage of its profits to the *locality*;

- that maximised its *local purchase* of goods and services or supported local *artisanal production*;
- sought to source its supplies *ethically*;
- minimised its *carbon footprint* or otherwise sought to be a *good environmental citizen*;
- thought through the implications of its purchasing for *supply chains*, and built these to achieve local or regional sustainability;
- *paid fairly, limited pay differentials*, and offered a *share in profits* to its employees;
- offered quality *training* to its employees; or
- sought to *devolve its decision making* to the local level, and involved a range of stakeholders.

These are just possibilities. As we have just noted, in a devolved experiment, socially-licensed policies and priorities would vary from place to place and context to context. However, whatever the salience of the individual items on the list, their diversity suggests that meaningful political engagement with the specifics in the economy will need to avoid losing sight of four principles.

- **Contestation.** Social concerns are *heterogeneous*. The list above includes employee, consumer, local, ethical, environmental, supply chain and organisational concerns. It is clear that these cannot be reduced to a single dimension. Inevitably there will be trade-offs, and equally inevitably there will be disagreements. There will be *no single right answer*.
- **Judgement.** Decisions about social licenses will therefore involve *irreducibly complex political and technical judgements* about priorities, preferred bidders, and appropriate organisational forms. Not only will algorithms never replace judgements, but those judgements will or should be more or less local and specific.
- **Discussion.** Judgements would or should be made *deliberatively, democratically* and *transparently*, though what this means will also be controversial. In particular, how expert advice can appropriately intersect with the concerns of consumers or citizens will vary, itself be contestable, and will be a proper matter for experiment.[8]
- **Tinkering.** Fourth, we may expect *judgements to change* with changing circumstances, priorities, and experience with existing experiments, successful and otherwise. In the complex world of social franchising no solution will ever be perfect, and the process will be one of social, economic and industrial tinkering (Mol 2008).

When the desiderata are laid out in this way, the problem becomes clear. None of these principles are unfamiliar. This kind of language has already been captured for reactionary purposes. Large companies have been pressured to consider their 'triple bottom line' (environmental and social, alongside financial), and many FTSE 100 corporations produce annual corporate social responsibility reports longer than this book outlining what they have done to manage the heterogeneous concerns of their various stakeholders in the workforce, supply chain and wider society. The thousands of pages of detailed consultation and economic modelling produced by quangos such as Ofcom and the Office of the Rail Regulator around seemingly minor regulatory decisions show there is no lack of technical sophistication in economic policy judgements. Central government departments, and many local authorities, are well versed in discourses about deliberative democracy and the necessity of broad engagement as an essential precondition of good policymaking. Our problem is that much of this represents a form of ritual and rhetoric that adds complexity without changing the arbitrary parameters of what types of economic interventions and behaviours are thinkable. In other words, it doesn't change the framing of economic action. And it is a change in that framing that we are seeking and that requires collective counter-pressure.

Changing the future together

Economic life and political life are experiments. And so, too, is the business of thinking, especially about alternatives. In this short book we have argued that British economic policy is an experiment that is failing because it has stopped learning, or learning well. Policy makers cannot question how they frame policy or think differently because they have been seized by a commitment to an abstraction – a particular version of competition, market and how to value transactions. Like the bedside physicians of the eighteenth century they are unwilling to let go of this. But this economic paralysis is also political. The centralising structures of the British state have rendered alternative experiments impossible. Economic abstraction has been coupled with power to impose that abstraction throughout the UK. The result has been a political economy that generates the conditions for its own failure in ways that are simultaneously intellectual, economic and institutional. 'There is no alternative framework', TINAF. So the non-learning goes on, along with the deterioration in working and living conditions.

But, if economic life and political life are interwoven experiments, then so too is the business of thinking, and the business of thinking alternatives. This means that the present book is an experiment. It rests upon solid research, and it draws on intellectual traditions which range from political science through history and political economy, to science, technology and society studies. But in the end we have developed an argument that is experimental in the sense that it is simultaneously new, incomplete, tentative, and open.

We have offered an alternative framing which attends to what we have called the foundational economy. This economic zone is important both for jobs and national prosperity, but is invisible within the current framing. Then, and politically, we have suggested that firms and sectors within the foundational economy should be understood as social licensees. Profit under private ownership should be just one part of a larger set of economic and social commitments and transactions. Firms and sectors should also be required to make a return, economic and otherwise: to the localities in which they operate; to their employees; to their consumers; to their supply chains; and to the broader social and natural environment. And then we have argued that this will only be possible if the central British state loosens its grip so that social licensing (and learning) can take various forms in different places. What works for one sector in London will not work in another sector in Swansea or Preston. In short, we will need to move from abstraction – from the idea that one size fits all in economic policy – to the kind of multiplicity pointed to by Braudel.

In all this, our larger aim has been to deny the inevitability of contemporary economic policy orthodoxy. If it turns out that the notion of the foundational economy and social licensing is helpful in rethinking policy then we will indeed be pleased. But more important has been the idea that Alternative Frameworks Are Possible (AFAP). Such would be our slogan with which to resist the TINAF orthodoxy. So, if reframing in terms of the foundational economy does not do the job, then we need to encourage alternative heterodox understandings of the complexity of economic life.

So the present book is an experiment and at the end of its argument we know that our intellectual and political ambitions exceed our grasp. The changes that are needed, whatever they may turn out to be, cannot be caught in a single book or by a single team of authors. Instead they will grow out of long-term and collaborative dialogue and experiment by the many who are both disempowered and represent the distributed intelligence of present day capitalism. Academics and many different kinds of experts will play a role, and so too will civil servants and activists, as well as corporate managers and trades unionists. Regional and local governments must play a leading role and so too must NGOs, voluntary organisations and other parts of civil society. All of these and more will need to play a role in the unfolding of a new set of economic experiments, and in new versions of learning. The collective challenges are daunting but, as this book shows in a small way, it is possible to work collaboratively and optimistically. While we can blame others for the continuing failure of the thirty year experiment, the political responsibility for ending that experiment and starting another is collectively ours. Our hope is that we can work on new experiments together.

Notes to Chapter 5

1 This chapter, like Chapter 1, has benefited from detailed comments and critique by John Buchanan of the Workplace Research Centre (WRC) at the University of Sydney. Some of our positions and arguments in this book overlap with those in earlier reports and articles from the WRC.
2 Our colleague, Ewald Engelen, was the first to insist on the relevance of Braudel to the foundational economy. The subsequent development of our position on Braudel is the result of internal team discussion, helped by a reading of Wallerstein's (1991) commentary.
3 Braudel's words resonate with findings from STS: there is no such thing as a single 'scientific method'. In practice science learns in different ways through different kinds of experiments and that is why it is so successful. The idea is implicit in Kuhn (1970). Much of modern economics is mono-method and suffers greatly in analytic purchase as a result.
4 We have recently analysed how this works in the case of the railway industry (see Bowman *et al.* 2013a).
5 The standard procedure is to discount future receipts at a given rate which is compounded year by year so that distant receipts are subject to multiple deductions and worth much less than receipts which are a year or two away. This depreciation of future earnings in a discounting calculation then works in reverse just like appreciation of current savings in a deposit account. A modest sum saved will be large after many years; so substantial earnings in the distant future will be worth little today. The algebra is impeccable, and the issue is about the universalisation of the calculative frame. It may be an appropriate decision principle for investment in a machine or factory, though Keynes would not agree. But, in our view, discounting should not be the basis for decision on major infrastructure and network projects like high speed rail or broadband where we have political options of ascertainable cost on an interconnected future where revenue and social benefits are both fundamentally uncertain over a long run of 50 years or more.

6 We owe the insistence on the relevance of American progressives to our French colleagues Valérie Revest and Véronique Dutraive. They also make a connection between social license and John Commons' concept of 'reasonable capitalism' (Dutraive and Revest 2011).

7 This point we owe to our businessman co–author Peter Folkman who argues that present day capitalist enterprise is often levered on a state which is financially embarrassed, as in early modern times.

8 There are considerable resources for thinking about in (for instance) participative technology policy. See Callon *et al.* (2009).

References

Armistead, L. (2013) 'BT chief hits out at "copper luddites" who hold back UK'. *Telegraph*, 7 April 2013.

Arthur, C. (2013) '4G auction to be investigated by audit office after poor return'. *Guardian*, 15 April 2013.

Ashton, J.K. (2009) 'Does the United Kingdom have regional banking markets? An assessment of UK deposit provision 1992–2006'. *Applied Economics Letters*, 16(11): 1123–8.

ATOC/ KPMG (2013) *Growth and Prosperity: How Franchising Helped Transform the Railway into a British Success Story.* Association of Train Operating Companies. Available at: http://www.atoc.org/latest-publications/ (accessed January 2014).

Bank of England (2013) *Trends in Lending October 2013*. London: Bank of England.

Barclays (2012) *Annual Report 2012*.

Barclays (2013a) 'Barclays plc. Becoming the go-to bank'. Presentation 12 February 2013. Available at: http://group.barclays.com/Satell ite?blobcol=urldata&blobheader=application%2Fpdf&blobheader name1=Content-Disposition&blobheadername2=MDT-Type&blo bheadervalue1=inline%3B+filename%3DAntony-Jenkins-presenta tion-to-investors-12-February-2013-PDF-1230.pdf&blobheaderval ue2=abinary%3B+charset%3DUTF-8&blobkey=id&blobtable=M ungoBlobs&blobwhere=1330696268998&ssbinary=true (accessed December 2013).

Barclays (2013b) *Becoming the 'Go-To' Bank. Barclays Strategic Review. Executive Summary*. Available at: http://group.barclays. com/mobile/about-barclays/about-us/transform/strategicreview (accessed December 2013).

Barclays (2013c) *Barclays PLC Strategic Review. Analyst Q&A Transcript, 12 February 2013*. Available at: http://group.barclays. com/Satellite?blobcol=urldata&blobheader=application%2Fpdf& blobheadername1=Content-Disposition&blobheadername2=MDT-Type&blobheadervalue1=inline%3B+filename%3DAnalyst-QA-

Transcript-PDF.pdf&blobheadervalue2=abinary%3B+charset%3
DUTF-8&blobkey=id&blobtable=MungoBlobs&blobwhere=1330
696773304&ssbinary=true

BBC (2000) 'The auction: winners and losers'. 27 April 2000. Available at: http://news.bbc.co.uk/1/hi/business/700180.stm (accessed January 2014).

BBC (2011a) 'Smartphone Britain: Ofcom's angst'. 10 October 2011. Available at: http://www.bbc.co.uk/news/technology-15237897 (accessed January 2014).

BBC (2011b) '"Stop fighting" MPs tell mobile operators'. 3 November 2011. Available at: http://www.bbc.co.uk/news/technology-15237897 (accessed January 2014).

BBC (2012a) 'UK is the most internet-based major economy'. 19 March 2012. Available at: http://www.bbc.co.uk/news/business-17405016 (accessed January 2014).

BBC (2012b) 'Rural broadband gets green light from Europe'. 10 October 2012. Available at: http://www.bbc.co.uk/news/technology-19882778 (accessed January 2014).

BBC (2013a) 'Rural broadband rollout: taxpayers being "ripped off", say MPs'. 26 September 2013. Available at: http://www.bbc.co.uk/news/technology-24227096 (accessed January 2014).

BBC (2013b) 'Tesco says almost 30,000 tonnes of food "wasted"'. 21 October 2013. Available at: http://www.bbc.co.uk/news/uk-24603008 (accessed December 2013).

BBC (2013c) 'Co-op Bank to cut branch network by at least 15%'. 4 November 2013. Available at: http://www.bbc.co.uk/news/business-24799513 (accessed December 2013).

BBC (2014) 'Labour plan to cap market share of High Street banks'. 15 January 2014. Available at http://www.bbc.co.uk/news/uk-politics-25737657 (accessed January 2014).

Bentham, J., Bowman, A., Froud, J., Johal, S., Leaver, A. and Williams, K. (2013) *Against New Industrial Strategy: Framing, Motifs and Absences*. Working Paper 126. University of Manchester: CRESC. Available at: http://www.cresc.ac.uk/people/prof-julie-froud

Berle, A. (1962) 'A new look at management responsibility'. Lecture to the Bureau of Industrial Relations, University of Michigan, 9 April 1962. Available at: http://3197d6d14b5f19f2f440-5e13d29c4c016cf96cbbfd197c579b45.r81.cf1.rackcdn.com/collection/papers/1960/1962_0409_ManagementBerleT.pdf (accessed January 2014).

Berle, A. and Means, G. (1932) *The Modern Corporation and Private Property*. New York: Macmillan.

Bevan, N. (1951) Resignation Speech, 23 April 1951. Available at http://www.sochealth.co.uk/national-health-service/the-sma-and-the-foundation-of-the-national-health-service-r-leslie-hilliard-1980/aneurinbevan-and-the-foundation-of-the-nhs/bevans-resignation-speech-23-april-1951/ (accessed January 2014).

Binmore, K. and Klemperer, P. (2002) 'The biggest auction ever: the sale of the British 3G telecom licences'. *The Economic Journal*, 112: C74-96.

Bond, M., Meacham, T., Bhunnoo, R. and Benton, T.G. (2013) *Food Waste Within Global Food Systems. A Global Food Security Report*. Swindon: Food Security.

Bose, P. and Morgan, A. (1998) 'Banking on shareholder value'. *McKinsey Quarterly*, 1998, No 2: 97–105.

Bowman, A., Froud, J., Johal, S., Law, J., Leaver, A. and Williams, K. (2012a) *Bringing Home the Bacon. From Trader Mentalities to Industrial Policy*. Manchester and Milton Keynes: CRESC. Available at: http://www.cresc.ac.uk/publications/bringing-home-the-bacon-from-trader-mentalities-to-industrial-policy (accessed December 2013).

Bowman, A., Ertürk, I., Froud, J., Johal, S., Law, J., Leaver, A., Moran, M. and Williams, K. (2012b) *The Finance and Point Value Complex*. Working Paper 118. Manchester and Milton Keynes: CRESC. Available at: http://www.cresc.ac.uk/publications/the-finance-and-point-value-complex (accessed January 2014).

Bowman, A., Folkman, P., Froud, J., Johal, S., Law, J., Leaver, A., Moran, M. and Williams, K. (2013a) *The Great Train Robbery: the Economic and Political Consequences of Rail Privatisation*. Manchester and Milton Keynes: CRESC. Available at: http://www.cresc.ac.uk/publications/the-great-train-robbery-the-economic-and-political-consequences-of-rail-privatisation (accessed January 2014).

Bowman, A., Folkman, P., Froud, J., Johal, S., Law, J., Leaver, A., Moran, M. and Williams, K. (2013b) *The Conceit of Enterprise: Train Operators and Trade Narrative*. Manchester and Milton Keynes: CRESC. Available at: http://www.cresc.ac.uk/sites/default/files/The%20Conceit%20of%20Enterprise.pdf (accessed December 2013).

Br0ken T3l3ph0n3 (2013) 'Red letter day for two rural broadband project'. Available at: http://br0kent3l3ph0n3.wordpress.com/2013/12/10/red-letter-day-for-two-rural-broadband-projects/ (accessed December 2013).

Bradey, J. (2013) 'What will retail banking look like in 2020?' *Bank Systems and Technology*. Available at: http://www.banktech.com/

channels/what-will-retail-banking-look-like-in-20/240149732 (accessed June 2013).

Braudel, F. (1981) *The Structures of Everyday Life. Civilization and Capitalism. Volume I.* (Tr: Sîan Renolds). New York: Harper and Row.

Braudel, F. (1982) *The Wheels of Commerce. Civilization and Capitalism Volume II.* (Tr: Sîan Reynolds). London: Collins.

Brigstocke, T. (2004) 'Future strategy for dairy farming in the UK'. *Journal of the Royal Agricultural Society of England*, vol 165.

British Bankers Association (2013) 'Bank support for smaller and medium sized enterprises'. 2 December 2013. Available at: http://www.bba.org.uk/statistics/article/banks-support-for-smes-quarter-3-2013/small-business/ (accessed December 2013).

Broadband Commission (2013) *The State of Broadband 2013: Universalizing Broadband: A report by the Broadband Commission: International Telecommunications Union / Unesco.* Available at http://www.broadbandcommission.org/Documents/bb-annualreport2013.pdf (accessed January 2014).

BSkyB (2012) *Annual Report and Accounts 2012.*

BSkyB (2013) *Annual Report and Accounts 2013.*

BT (2012) 'Superfast broadband: boosting business and the UK economy. Available at: http://www.btplc.com/Thegroup/BTUKandWorldwide/BTRegions/England/Factsandfigures/Superfast-broadband.pdf (accessed January 2014).

BT (2013) 'BT Group plc Q2 2013/14 Results Presentation Transcript, 31 October 2013'. Available at: http://www.btplc.com/Sharesandperformance/Quarterlyresults/PDFdownloads/q213_transcript.pdf (accessed January 2014).

BT (2014a) 'BT archives: events in telecommunications history'. Available at: http://www.btplc.com/thegroup/btshistory/1912to1968/1966.htm (accessed January 2014).

BT (2014b) 'Q3 2013/14 results'. Available at: https://www.btplc.com/Sharesandperformance/Quarterlyresults/PDFdownloads/q314-slides.pdf (accessed January 2014).

BT (undated) 'The historical development of BT'. Available at: http://www.btplc.com/Thegroup/BTsHistory/History.htm (accessed January 2014).

Buchanan, J., Dymski, G., Froud, J., Johal, S., Leaver, A. and Williams, K. (2013) 'Unsustainable employment portfolios'. *Work Employment & Society*, 27(3): 396–413.

Burr Williams, J. (1938) *The Theory of Investment Value.* Harvard, MA: Harvard University Press.

Callon, M., Lascoumes, P. and Barthe, Y. (2009) *Acting in an Uncertain World: an Essay on Technical Democracy*. Cambridge, Mass., and London: MIT Press.

Carsberg, B. (1986) 'Regulating private monopolies and promoting competition'. *Long Range Planning*, 19(6): 75–81.

Chazen, G. (2014) 'UK power distribution companies complacent in storm response'. *Financial Times*, 21 January 2014.

Churm, R., Radia, A., Leake, J., Srinivasan, S. and Whisker, R. (2012) 'The funding for lending scheme'. *Bank of England Quarterly Bulletin*, 2012 Q4: 306–20.

Citizens Advice (2005) 'Protection racket. CAB evidence on the cost and effectiveness of payment protection insurance'. Available at: http://www.citizensadvice.org.uk/index/policy/policy_publica tions/er_credit_debt/protection_racket.htm (accessed December 2013).

Commission for Rural Communities (2010a) 'Rural mobile phone coverage – issues and recommendations'. Available at: http:// webarchive.nationalarchives.gov.uk/20101121101601/http:/rural communities.gov.uk/wp-content/uploads/2010/11/ruralmobilecov erage.pdf (accessed January 2014).

Commission for Rural Communities (2010b) *Rural Advocate Report*. London: Department for Environment, Farming and Rural Affairs.

Competition Commission (2008) *The Supply of Groceries in the UK: Market Investigation*. Available at http://www.competition-commission.org.uk/assets/competitioncommission/docs/pdf/non-inquiry/rep_pub/reports/2008/fulltext/538 (accessed January 2014).

Crafts, N. (2011a) 'Competition cured the "British Disease"' *Vox*, 5 June 2011. Available at: http://www.voxeu.org/article/competition-cured-british-disease (accessed December 2013).

Crafts, N. (2011b) *British Relative Economic Decline Revisited*. Centre for Economic Policy Research Discussion Paper 8384. London: Centre for Economic Policy Research.

CRESC (2009) *An Alternative Report on UK Banking Reform*. Manchester and Milton Keynes: Centre for Research in Socio-Cultural Change. Available at: http://www.cresc.ac.uk/ publications/an-alternative-report-on-uk-banking-reform (accessed January 2014).

Cruickshank, D. (2000) *Competition in UK Banking: a Report to the Chancellor of the Exchequer*. London: The Stationery Office.

Cutler, T., Haslam, C., Williams, J. and Williams, K. (1989) *1992: The Struggle for Europe*. Oxford: Berg Publishers.

Dairy Crest (2013) *Annual Report and Accounts*.

Dairy UK, NFU and NFU Scotland (2012) *Dairy Industry. Code of Good Practice on Contractual Relations*. Available at: http://www. nfuonline.com/assets/6570 (accessed December 2013).

DairyCo (2012a) *Profiting From Efficient Milk Production*. Available at: http://www.dairyco.org.uk/non_umbraco/download. aspx?media=11427 (accessed December 2013).

DairyCo (2012b) *Milk Calculator and Contacts. League Table*. http://www.dairyco.org.uk/market-information/milk-prices-contr acts/milk-calculator-and-contracts/league-tables/ (accessed January 2014).

DairyCo (2012c) *Dairy Statistics: An Insider's Guide 2012*. Available at: http://www.dairyco.org.uk/resources-library/market-information/dairy-statistics/dairy-statistics-an-insider's-guide-2012/ (accessed January 2014).

DairyCo (2012d) *Dairy Supply Chain Margins 2011/12*. Available at: http://www.dairyco.org.uk/resources-library/market-information/ dairy-supply-chain-reports/dairy-supply-chain-margins-2012/#.Uv DKtSpdyUk (accessed December 2013).

DairyCo (2013a) *The Structure of the GB Dairy Farming Industry – What Drives Change?* Available at: http://www.dairyco.org.uk/ resources-library/market-information/industry-structure/the-struc ture-of-the-gb-dairy-farming-industry-what-drives-change/#.UvDK 6SpdyUk (accessed December 2013).

DairyCo (2013b) *Guide to Milk Buyers: a Review of Strategy and Performance 2013*. Available at: http://www.dairyco.org.uk/ resources-library/market-information/company-strategy-performa nce-report/guide-to-milk-buyers-2013/#.UvDJwSpdyUk (accessed January 2014).

DairyCo (2013c) *Cheddar Supply Margins 2013*. Available at: http://www.dairyco.org.uk/resources-library/market-information/ dairy-supply-chain-reports/cheddar-supply-chain-margins-report-201213/#.UvDKLipdyUk (accessed December 2013).

DEFRA (2010) *Definitions of Terms used in Farm Business Management*. Available at: http://www.neat-network.eu/sites/neat-network. eu/files/Definition%20of%20terms.pdf (accessed January 2014).

DEFRA (2013) *Farm Business Income by Type of Farm in England, 2012/13*. Available at: https://www.gov.uk/government/uploads/sys tem/uploads/attachment_data/file/266051/Farm_Business_Income_ 2012_13.pdf (accessed January 2014).

Dellis, J., Amjad, N., Rathe, U. and Thorne, G. (2013) *BT plc: FCF Outlook Warrants Premium Rating*. Jeffries: Company Note.

Deloitte (2007). *Winning with Branches*. London: Deloitte LLP.

Department for Business, Innovation and Skills (2010) *Britain's Superfast Broadband Future*. Available at: https://www.gov.uk/gov ernment/uploads/system/uploads/attachment_data/file/78096/10-1320-britains-superfast-broadband-future.pdf (accessed January 2014).

Department for Business, Innovation and Skills (2013) 'Building the business bank'. London: BIS. Available at: https://www.gov.uk/government/uploads/system/uploads/attachment_data/file/203148/bis-13-734-building-the-business-bank-strategy-march-2013.pdf (accessed December 2013).

Department for Business, Innovation and Skills (2014) *Preventing and Reducing Anti-competitive Activities*. Available at: https://www.gov.uk/government/policies/preventing-and-reducing-anti-competi tive-activities (accessed January 2014).

Department for Culture, Media and Sport (2012) 'Ten super-connected cities announced'. Available at: https://www.gov.uk/government/news/ten-super-connected-cities-announced (accessed January 2014).

Department for Culture, Media and Sport (2013) 'Broadband delivery UK: details of the plan to achieve a transformation in broadband in the UK by 2015'. Available at: https://www.gov.uk/broadband-delivery-uk (accessed January 2014).

Department for Environment, Food and Rural Affairs (2012) *Food Statistics Pocketbook*. London: DEFRA.

Department for Trade and Industry (1988) *Information Technology. Government's Response to the First Report of the House of Commons Trade and Industry Committee*. 1988–89 session. CM 646. London: Stationery Office.

Department for Trade and Industry (1991) *Competition and Choice: Telecommunications Policy for the 1990s*. Cmnd 1461. London: HMSO.

Dutraive, V. and Revest, V. (2011) 'La régulation des relations finance-industrie: capitalisme responsable ou raisonnable?' *Revue d'Economie Financière*, 104: 125–38.

Engelen, E., Ertürk, I., Froud, J., Johal, S., Leaver, A., Moran, M., Nilsson, A. and Williams, K. (2011) *After the Great Complacence*. Oxford: Oxford University Press.

Ertürk, I. (2012) 'Make the break: why ring-fencing falls short and full separation is a necessary first step for British banks'. Report No. 309. London: Good Banking Forum.

Ertürk, I., Froud, J., Johal, S., Leaver, A. and Williams, K. (2008) *Financialization at Work*. London: Routledge.

Ertürk, I., Froud, J., Johal, S., Leaver, A., Moran, M. and Williams, K. (2011) *City State Against National Settlement UK Economic Policy and Politics After the Financial Crisis*. Working Paper no.101. Manchester and Milton Keynes: CRESC. Available at: http://www.cresc.ac.uk/publications/city-state-against-national-settlement-uk-economic-policy-and-politics-after-the-financial-crisis (accessed December 2013).

Esping Andersen, G. (1990) *The Three Worlds of Welfare Capitalism*. Princeton NJ: Princeton University Press.

European Commission (2012) *Evolution of the Market Situation and the Consequent Conditions for Smoothly Phasing out the Milk Quota System – Second 'Soft Landing' Report*. Available at: http://ec.europa.eu/agriculture/milk/quota-report/com-2012-741_en.pdf (accessed January 2014).

European Commission (undated) 'Broadband: inter-institutional negotiations on the Connected Europe Facility'. Available at: http://ec.europa.eu/dgs/connect/en/content/broadband-inter-instit utional-negotiations-connected-europe-facility (accessed January 2014).

European Parliament (2000) *EC Regulation on Local Loop Unbundling* (EC/2887/2000). Available at: http://eur-lex.europa. eu/LexUriServ/LexUriServ.do?uri=OJ:L:2000:336:0004:0004:EN: PDF (accessed January 2014).

FCA (2013) 'Final notice'. 10 December 2013. Available at: http:// www.fca.org.uk/static/documents/final-notices/lloyds-tsb-bank-and-bank-of-scotland.pdf (accessed December 2013).

Financial Ombudsman Service (2013) 'Consumer factsheet on payment protection insurance'. Available at: http://www.financial-ombudsman.org.uk/publications/factsheets/payment-protection-insurance.pdf (accessed December 2013).

Ford, R. (2011) 'Asda's milk premium to farmers cut by 20%'. *The Grocer*, 24 October 2011.

Foreman-Peck, J. & Manning, D. (1988) 'How well is BT perform-ing? An international comparison of telecommunications total factor productivity'. *Fiscal Studies* 9(3): 54–67.

Foreman-Peck, J. (1985) 'Competition and performance in the UK telecommunications industry'. *Telecommunications Policy*, September 1985.

Friends of the Earth (2005) 'How to oppose a supermarket plan-ning application'. Available at: http://www.foe.co.uk/sites/default/files/downloads/campaigning_against_supermarkets.pdf (accessed January 2014).

Froud, J. Johal, S., Leaver, A., Phillips, R. and Williams, K. (2009) 'Stressed by choice: a business model analysis of the BBC'. *British Journal of Management*, 20(2): 252–64.

Froud, J., Johal, S., Leaver, A, and Williams, K. (2014) 'Financialization across the Pacific: manufacturing cost ratios, supply chains and power'. *Critical Perspectives on Accounting*, 25(1): 46–57.

FSA (2005) 'The sale of payment protection insurance – results of thematic work'. Available at: http://www.fsa.gov.uk/pubs/other/ppi_thematic_report.pdf (accessed December 2013).

FSA (2012) 'What is payment protection insurance?' Available at: http://www.fsa.gov.uk/consumerinformation/product_news/insurance/payment_protection_insurance_/what-is-ppi (accessed December 2013).

FTTH Council Europe (2013) 'Winners and losers emerge in Europe's race to a fibre future'. http://www.ftthcouncil.eu/documents/PressReleases/2013/PR2013_EU_Ranking_FINAL.pdf (accessed January 2014).

Garside, J. (2012a) 'Whistleblower sacked over BT rural broadband leak'. *Guardian*, 3 October 2012.

Garside, J. (2012b) Virgin Media and BT take legal action against Birmingham council broadband, *The Guardian* 21 October 2012.

Gillandes, E. (2013) 'Groceries code adjudicator opts to tread carefully'. *Farmers Weekly*, 11 November 2013.

Gilmour, I. (1992) *Dancing With Dogma*. London: Simon and Schuster.

Goff, S. (2013) 'Nationwide steps back from SME loans'. *Financial Times*, 26 August 2013.

Gordon, R.J. (2012) 'Is US economic growth over? Faltering innovation confronts the six headwinds'. Working Paper 18315, National Bureau of Economic Research. Cambridge MA: NBER.

Graham, B. (1939) 'The theory of investment value, by John Burr Williams'. *Journal of Political Economy*, 47(2): 276–8.

Groceries Code Adjudicator (2013a) *Groceries Code Adjudicator: Supporting Facts With Questions and Answers*. Available at: https://www.gov.uk/government/uploads/system/uploads/attachment_data/file/226119/GCA_Supporting_facts_and_QAs_July_2013.pdf (accessed January 2014).

Groceries Code Adjudicator (2013b) *Statutory Guidance on How the Groceries Code Adjudicator Will Carry out Investigation and Enforcement Functions*. Available at: https://www.gov.uk/government/uploads/system/uploads/attachment_data/file/226054

/31_July_2013_-_GCA_Statutory_Guidance_for_consultation.pdf (accessed January 2014).

Gustavsson, J., Cederberg, C. and Sonesson, U. (2011) *Global Food Losses and Food Waste*. Rome: FAO. Available at: http://www. fao.org/fileadmin/user_upload/suistainability/pdf/Global_Food_ Losses_and_Food_Waste.pdf (accessed January 2014).

Hawkins, O. (2011) *Dairy Industry UK: Statistics – Commons Library Standard Note*. Available at: http://www.parliament.uk/ briefing-papers/SN02721/dairy-industry-uk-statistics (accessed January 2014).

HBOS (2001) *Annual Report and Accounts 2011*.

HM Treasury (2011) 'Government welcomes banks' statements on lending 15% more to SMEs, and on pay and support for regional growth'. News Release, 9 February 2011. Available at: https:// www.gov.uk/government/news/government-welcomes-banks-state ments-on-lending-15-more-to-smes-and-on-pay-and-support-for- regional-growth (accessed December 2013).

HM Treasury (2012) *Review into HM Treasury's Management of the Financial Crisis*. London: HM Treasury. Available at: https://www. gov.uk/government/news/review-into-hm-treasurys-management- of-the-financial-crisis--2 (accessed December 2013).

HM Treasury (2013a) 'Bank of England and HM Treasury re- focus the Funding for Lending Scheme to support business lending in 2014'. News Release, 28 November 2013. Available at: https://www.gov.uk/government/news/bank-of-england-and- hm-treasury-re-focus-the-funding-for-lending-scheme-to-support- business-lending-in-2014 (accessed December 2013).

HM Treasury (2013b) Investing in Britain's future. Available at: https://www.gov.uk/government/uploads/system/uploads/attach ment_data/file/209279/PU1524_IUK_new_template.pdf (accessed January 2014).

House of Commons Culture Media and Sport Committee (2011) 'Culture, Media and Sport Committee backs Spectrum auction in new report'. Press release, 3 November 2011. Available at: http:// www.parliament.uk / business / committees / committees - a - z / com mons-select/culture-media-and-sport-committee/news/committee- publishes-report-on-spectrum/ (accessed December 2013).

House of Commons Environment, Food and Rural Affairs Committee (2012) *Milk Pricing – Minutes of Evidence*. HC 538. London: The Stationery Office. Available at: http://www.publications. parliament.uk/pa/cm201213/cmselect/cmenvfru/538/120717.htm (accessed January 2014).

House of Commons Public Accounts Committee (2011) *Lessons From PFI and Other Projects*. 44th Report Session 2010-12. HC 1201. London: The Stationery Office.

House of Commons Public Accounts Committee (2013a) *The Rural Broadband Programme*. 24th report volume I, session 2013-14. HC 474.

House of Commons Public Accounts Committee (2013b) 'Committee publishes report on the Rural Broadband programme'. Available at: http://www.parliament.uk/business/committees/committees-a-z/commons-select/public-accounts-committee/news/rural-broad band-report/ (accessed January 2014).

House of Commons Trade and Industry Committee (2005) *Ofcom's Strategic Review of Telecommunications*. Thirteenth Report Session 2004–05. London: The Stationery Office. Available at: http://www.publications.parliament.uk/pa/cm200405/cmselect/cmtrdind/407/407.pdf (accessed January 2014).

House of Commons Welsh Affairs Committee (2013) *The Voluntary Code of Practice in the Dairy Sector*. First Report Session 2013–14, Volume I. London: The Stationery Office. Available at: http://www.publications.parliament.uk/pa/cm201314/cmselect/cm welaf/155/155.pdf (accessed January 2014).

House of Lords Select Committee on Communication (2012) *Broadband For All—an Alternative Vision*. 1st Report Session 2012–13. London: The Stationery Office. Available at: http://www.publications.parliament.uk/pa/ld201213/ldselect/ldcomuni/41/41.pdf (accessed January 2014).

Howard, S., Minerva, L., Cote-Colisson, N., Klarmann, D. and Rumley, A. (2012) 'Four steps for fibre: how to secure Europe's super-fast broadband future'. London: HSBC. December 2012.

Hughes, S. (2013) 'Britain is failing the broadband test'. *Local Government Chronicle*, 13 August 2013. Available at http://www.lgcplus.com/briefings/britain-is-failing-the-broadband-test/50622 06.article (accessed January 2014).

IMF (2013) 'United Kingdom—2013 Article IV consultation. Concluding statement of the Mission'. 22 May 2013. Available at: http://www.imf.org/external/np/ms/2013/052213.htm (accessed January 2014).

Independent Commission on Banking (2011) *Final Report. Recommendations*. Available at: https://hmt-sanctions.s3.amazon aws.com/ICB%20final%20report/ICB%2520Final%2520Report%5B1%5D.pdf (accessed December 2013).

Independent Networks Cooperative Association (2013) 'Public

Accounts Committee: written evidence from the Independent Networks Cooperative Association (INCA)'. Available at: http://www.publications.parliament.uk/pa/cm201314/cmselect/cmpubacc/474/474vw04.htm (accessed January 2014).

Institution of Mechanical Engineers (2013) *Global Food: Waste Not, Want Not*. London: IME. Available at: http://www.imeche.org/docs/default-source/reports/Global_Food_Report.pdf?sfvrsn=0 (accessed January 2014).

Jenkins, P. (2013) 'Co-op advisers did not assess Britannia's corporate loans'. *Financial Times*, 3 December 2013.

Jenkins, P., Schäfer, D. and Thompson, J. (2013) 'Evangelism belies change at Barclays'. *Financial Times*, 12 February 2013.

Jewson, N. (1976) 'The disappearance of the sick-man from medical cosmology, 1770–1870'. *Sociology*, 10(2): 225–44.

Johnson, B. (2013) *The 2013 Margaret Thatcher Lecture*. Centre for Policy Studies, 27 November 2013. Available at: http://www.cps.org.uk/events/q/date/2013/11/27/the-2013-margaret-thatcher-lecture-boris-johnson/ (accessed January 2014).

Kavanagh, M. (2010) 'Price battles prompt Robert Wiseman warning'. *Financial Times*, 17 September 2010.

Kay, J. (2009) 'Banks must learn to put the customer first'. *The Daily Telegraph*, 16 September 2009.

Key Note (2012) *Milk and Dairy Products Market Report*. Teddington: Key Note Ltd.

Keynes, J.M. (1936) *The General Theory*. London: Palgrave Macmillan.

King, A. and Crewe, I. (2013) *The Blunders of our Governments*. London: Oneworld Publications.

King, M. (2013) Speech given at the CBI Northern Ireland Mid-Winter Dinner, Belfast, 22 January 2013. Available at: http://www.bankofengland.co.uk/publications/Documents/speeches/2013/speech631.pdf (accessed January 2014).

Knight, F. (1921) *Risk, Uncertainty and Profit*. Boston, MA: Houghton Mifflin.

KPMG (2013) *UK Banks: Performance Benchmarking Report*. London: KPMG.

Kuhn, T.S. (1970) *The Structure of Scientific Revolutions*. Chicago: Chicago University Press.

Kwoka, J.E. (1993) 'The effects of divestiture, privatization, and competition on productivity in US and UK telecommunications'. *Review of Industrial Organization*, 8: 49–61.

Labour Party (2013) *Powering Britain: One Nation Labour's Plans to Reset the Energy Market*. London: Labour Party. Available at:

http://www.yourbritain.org.uk/agenda-2015/policy-review/policy-review/energy-green-paper (accessed January 2014).

Lamond, F.E. (1978) 'The UK telecommunications monopoly: an independent view'. *Telecommunications Policy*, September 1978: 209–16.

Langdale, J. (1982) 'Competition in telecommunications'. *Telecommunications Policy*, 6(4): 283–99.

Large, A. (2013) *RBS Independent Lending Review*. Available at: http://www.independentlendingreview.co.uk/index.htm (accessed December 2013).

Law, J. and Williams, K. (2014) *A State of Unlearning? Government as Experiment*. CRESC Working Paper 134, Manchester and Milton Keynes: CRESC. Available at: http://www.cresc.ac.uk/publications/a-state-of-unlearning-government-as-experiment (accessed January 2014).

Lazonick, W. and O'Sullivan, M. (2000) 'Maximising shareholder value: a new ideology for corporate governance'. *Economy and Society*, 29(1): 13–35.

Leach, A. (2012) 'BT and Virgin sue over £10m state-funded Birmingham broadband'. *The Register*, 22 October 2012. Available at: http://www.theregister.co.uk/2012/10/22/bt_virgin_media_birmingham_broadband/ (accessed January 2014).

Lex (2014) 'Sainsbury: King leaves UK supermarket'. *Financial Times*, 29 January 2014.

Lucas, L. (2012) 'Dairy Crest loses Tesco contract'. *Financial Times*, 17 April 2012.

Mackenzie, G. (2013a) 'AFMP dairy farmers set for full Arla membership'. *Farmers Weekly*, 30 August 2013.

Mackenzie, G. (2013b) 'Dairy processors – the big four in the spotlight'. *Farmers Weekly*, 14 October 2013.

Macmillan, H. (1938) *The Middle Way*. London: Macmillan.

Massoudi, A. and Lucas, L. (2010) 'Müller to buy Robert Wiseman for £279m'. *Financial Times*, 16 January 2010.

Mazzucato, M. (2013) *The Entrepreneurial State*. London: Anthem Press.

Miningfacts.org (undated) 'What is the social license to operate (SLO)?'. Available at: http://www.miningfacts.org/Communities/What-is-the-social-licence-to-operate/ (accessed January 2014).

Mintel (2013a) *Packaged and Current Accounts: July 2013*. London: Mintel.

Mintel (2013b) *Small Business Banking: December 2013*. London: Mintel.

Mitchell, T. (1998) 'Fixing the economy'. *Cultural Studies*, 12(1): 82–101.

Mitchell, T. (2002) *Rule of Experts: Egypt, Techno-Politics, Modernity*. Berkeley: University of California Press.

Mitchell, T. (2008) 'Rethinking economy'. *Geoforum* 39: 1116–21.

Mol, A. (2008) *The Logic of Care: Health and the Problem of Patient Choice*. London: Routledge.

Moore, E. (2014) 'Post Office extends bank services'. *Financial Times*, 13 January 2014.

Moran, M. (1999) *Governing the Health Care State: a Comparative Study of the United Kingdom, United States and Germany*. Manchester: Manchester University Press.

Moran, M. (2007) *The British Regulatory State: High Modernism and Hyper-Innovation*. Oxford: Oxford University Press.

Morgan, I. (2008) 'We are going to "Tredegar-ise" you, Bevan told rest of the UK'. *WalesOnline*, 5 March 2008. Available at: http://www.walesonline.co.uk/news/health/going-tredegar-ise-you-bevan-told-2187499 (accessed January 2014).

NAO (2011) *Lessons From PFI and Other Projects*. Session 2010–2012. HC 920. London: The Stationery Office.

NAO (2013) *The Rural Broadband Programme*. House of Commons Paper HC 535, 2013–14. London: The Stationery Office.

Nias, B. (2013) 'TSB launches with £30m multi-channel campaign'. *Campaign*, 9 September 2013. Available at: http://www.campaignlive.co.uk/news/1210959/ (accessed December 2013).

Nimmo, R. (2010) *Milk, Modernity and the Making of the Human: Purifying the Social*. Abingdon, New York: Routledge.

Nussbaum, M. (2000) *Women and Human Development: The Capabilities Approach*. Cambridge: Cambridge University Press.

OECD (2012) 'Broadband portal'. Available at: http://www.oecd.org/sti/broadband/oecdbroadbandportal.htm#Services_and_speeds (accessed January 2014).

Ofcom (1999) 'Access to bandwidth: delivering competition for the information age. A statement issued by the Director General of Telecommunications'. Available at: http://www.ofcom.org.uk/static/archive/oftel/publications/1999/consumer/a2b1199.htm (accessed January 2014).

Ofcom (2004) *Strategic Review of Telecommunications: Phase 2 Consultation Document*. Available at: http://stakeholders.ofcom.org.uk/binaries/consultations/telecoms_p2/summary/maincondoc.pdf (accessed January 2014).

Ofcom (2005a) 'Universal service obligation: a review'. Available at: http://stakeholders.ofcom.org.uk/consultations/uso/main/ (accessed January 2014).

Ofcom (2005b) 'Final statements on the Strategic Review of Telecommunications, and undertakings in lieu of a reference under the Enterprise Act 2002'. Available at: http://stakeholders. ofcom.org.uk/binaries/consultations/752417/statement/statement. pdf (accessed January 2014).

Ofcom (2005c) 'Ofcom's approach to risk in the assessment of the cost of capital'. Available at: http://stakeholders.ofcom.org.uk/ binaries/consultations/cost_capital2/statement/final.pdf (accessed January 2014).

Ofcom (2010) 'Review of the wholesale broadband access markets'. Available at: http://stakeholders.ofcom.org.uk/consultations/wba/ wba-statement/ (accessed January 2014).

Ofcom (2012a) *International Communications Market Report 2012*. Available at: http://stakeholders.ofcom.org.uk/binaries/research/ cmr/cmr12/icmr/ICMR-2012.pdf (accessed January 2014).

Ofcom (2012b) *The Consumer Experience of 2013: Telecoms, Internet, Digital Broadcasting and Post*. Available at: http://stakeholders. ofcom.org.uk/binaries/research/consumer-experience/tce-13/TCE_ Policy_Final.pdf (accessed January 2014).

Ofcom (2013a) *Communications Market Report 2013*, London: Ofcom.

Ofcom (2013b) 'Fixed access market reviews: approach to setting LLU and WLR charge controls'. Available at: http://stakeholders. ofcom.org.uk/consultations/llu-wlr-cc-13/ (accessed January 2014).

Ofcom (2013c) 'Complaint from TalkTalk Telecom Group plc against BT Group plc about alleged margin squeeze in superfast broad-band pricing'. Available at: http://stakeholders.ofcom.org.uk/ enforcement/competition-bulletins/open-cases/all-open-cases/cw_ 01103/ (accessed January 2014).

Ofcom (2013d) 'New measures to boost superfast broadband competition'. Available at: http://media.ofcom.org.uk/2013/07/03/ new-measures-to-boost-superfast-broadband-competition/ (accessed January 2014).

Ofcom (2013e) 'Average UK broadband speed continues to rise'. Available at: http://media.ofcom.org.uk/2013/08/07/average-uk-broadband-speed-continues-to-rise/ (accessed January 2014).

Ofcom (2013f) 'Ensuring 3G coverage compliance'. Available at: http://media.ofcom.org.uk/2013/11/07/ensuring-3g-coverage-com pliance/ (accessed January 2014).

Ofcom (2014) *The Consumer Experience of 2013: Telecoms, Internet, Digital Broadcasting and Post*. Available at http://stakeholders. ofcom.org.uk/binaries/research/consumer-experience/tce-13/TCE_ Policy_Final.pdf (accessed January 2014).

Ofcom (undated a) 'Broadband speeds – consumer Q&A'. Available at: http://stakeholders.ofcom.org.uk/telecoms/codes-of-practice/ broadband-speeds-cop/faqs/ (accessed January 2014).

Ofcom (undated b) 'What is Local-Loop unbundling?' Available at: http://www.ofcom.org.uk/static/archive/oftel/publications/ broadband/dsl_facts/LLUbackground.htm (accessed January 2014).

Office for National Statistics (2012) *Family Spending. 2012 Edition*. Available at: http://www.ons.gov.uk/ons/rel/family-spending/ family-spending/family-spending-2012-edition/index.html (accessed December 2013).

OFT (2005) 'Response to the super-complaint on payment protection insurance made by Citizens Advice'. Available at: http:// www.oft.gov.uk/shared_oft/super-complaints/oft825.pdf (accessed December 2013).

OFT (2006) *Payment Protection Insurance. Report on the Market Study and Proposed Decision to Make a Market Investigation Reference*. London: OFT.

OFT (2008) *Personal Current Accounts in the UK – An OFT Market Study*. London: The Office of Fair Trading.

OFT (2009) *Government in Markets. Why Competition Matters – a Guide for Policy Makers*. London: OFT. Available at: http:// www.oft.gov.uk/shared_oft/business_leaflets/general/OFT1113.pdf (accessed December 2013).

OFT (2013) *Review of the Personal Current Account Market*. London: Office of Fair Trading.

Parker, D. (2009) *The Official History of Privatisation Vol. I: the Formative Years 1970–1987*. London: Routledge.

Parliamentary Commission on Banking Standards (2012a) 'Written evidence from the Competition Commission'. Available at: http:// www.publications.parliament.uk/pa/jt201314/jtselect/jtpcbs/27/27 ix_we_j10.htm (accessed December 2013).

Parliamentary Commission on Banking Standards (2012b) 'Written evidence from Clive Briault'. Available at: http://www.publications. parliament.uk/pa/jt201314/jtselect/jtpcbs/27/27ix_we_j19.htm (accessed December 2013).

Parliamentary Commission on Banking Standards (2013a) *'An Accident Waiting to Happen': The Failure of HBOS*. 4th Report,

Volume 1, Session 2013–14. House of Lords Paper 27/ House of Commons Paper 175. London: The Stationery Office.

Parliamentary Commission on Banking Standards (2013b) *Changing Banking For Good*. 5th Report, Session 2012–13. House of Lords Paper 144/ House of Commons Paper 705. London: The Stationery Office.

Parsons, R. (2012) 'Barclays promises a "relentless customer focus" to rebuild trust'. *Marketing Week*, 6 December 2012. Available at: http://www.marketingweek.co.uk/news/barclays-promises-a-relentless-customer-focus-to-rebuild-trust/4005044.article (accessed December 2013).

Patrick, M., Bishop, M., Dann, J. and Davids, J.P. (2013) *BT Group PLC: FibrEconomics*. London: Barclays Equity Research.

Payments Council (undated) 'Account switching explained'. Available at: http://www.paymentscouncil.org.uk/switch_service/account_switching_explained/ (accessed December 2013).

Peel Hunt (2013) *Dairy Crest: The Whey Forward*. 19 September 2013. London: Peel Hunt.

Perkin, H. (2003) *The Rise of Professional Society: England since 1880*. London: Routledge.

Peston, R. (2014) 'Labour to force bank break-ups'. 16 January 2014. Available at http://www.bbc.co.uk/news/business-25768906 (accessed January 2014).

Polanyi, K. (1944) *The Great Transformation*. New York: Farrar & Rinehart.

Power, M. (1997) *The Audit Society: Rituals of Verification*. Oxford: Oxford University Press.

Pye, R. (1978) 'Telecommunications and the UK government'. *Telecommunications Policy*, December 1978: 339–441.

Pye, R., Heath, M., Spring, G. and Yeoman, J. (1991) 'Competition and choice in telecommunications: the duopoly review consultative document'. *Telecommunications Policy*, February 1991: 10–14.

Quarry, J., Low, S., Hill, G. and Baveja, R. (2012) *Perspectives on the UK Retail Banking Market*. London: Oliver Wyman.

Quiggan, J. (2010) *Zombie Economics: How Dead Ideas Still Walk Among Us*. Princeton NJ: Princeton University Press.

Read, S. (2013) 'British Gas fuel price hike: David Cameron faces backlash after advising customers to change supplier'. *The Independent*, 17 October 2013.

Roch, J. (2013) *UK Telecom and Media: BT/BSkyB Wholesale dynamics*. London: Barclays Equity Research.

Russell, M. (2012) 'Dairy farmers single out retailers at Yorkshire show'. *just-food*, 11 July 2012. Available at: http://www.just-food.com/the-just-food-blog/dairy-farmers-single-out-retailers-at-yorkshire-show_id2251.aspx (accessed January 2014).

Salz Review (2013) *An Independent Review of Barclays' Business Practices*. Available at: https://www.salzreview.co.uk/c/document_library/get_file?uuid=557994c9-9c7f-4037-887b-8b5623bed25e&groupId=4705611 (accessed December 2013).

Sarangi, A. (2006) *Northern Rock: This Train has Left the Station*. ING Equity Markets Report, 19 September 2006. London: ING.

Scott, J. (1999) *Seeing Like a State*. Yale, CT: Yale University Press.

Searle, G. (1971) *The Quest for National Efficiency: a Study in British Politics and Political Thought*. London: University of California Press.

Sen, A. (1985) *Commodities and Capabilities*. Oxford: Oxford University Press.

Shah, D. (2013) 'Analysts divided on Barclays'. *Money Observer*, 12 February 2013. Available at: http://www.moneyobserver.com/news/12-02-2013/analysts-divided-barclays (accessed December 2013).

Sidney, P. (2013) *BT Group: Increase Target Price*. London: Credit Suisse Equity Research.

Socialicense (undated) 'The social license to operate'. Available at: http://socialicense.com/ (accessed January 2014).

Solomon, J.H. (1986) 'Telecommunications evolution in the UK'. *Telecommunications Policy*, September 1986: 186–92.

TalkTalk (2008) 'A new pricing framework for Openreach: second consultation'. London: TalkTalk Group. Available at: http://stakeholders.ofcom.org.uk/binaries/consultations/openreachframework/responses/Talk_Talk_Group.pdf (accessed January 2014).

TalkTalk (2013) *Annual Report and Accounts 2013*.

Tebbit, N. (1991) *Unfinished Business*. London: Weidenfeld and Nicholson.

Tesco (2013) 'Report from the Chief Executive. Annual Review 2013'. Available at: http://www.tescoplc.com/index.asp?pageid=544 (accessed January 2014).

Tesco (2014) *Our Milk*. Available at: http://realfood.tesco.com/our-food/milk/our-milk.html (accessed January 2014).

Thomas, D. (2013) 'TalkTalk seeks BT network regulation'. *Financial Times*, 31 March 2013.

Thompson, J. (2013) 'Ditching Lloyds branches deal leaves Co-op with other challenges'. *Financial Times*, 24 April 2013.

Thompson, J., Jenkins, P. and Powley, T. (2013) 'Nationwide faces £2bn shortfall after "crude" test'. *Financial Times*, 21 June 2013.

Thomson Reuters (2013) 'Q2 and half year results 2013/14 BT Group PLC earnings conference call'. London: Thomson Reuters.

Tomlinson, L. (2013) *Banks' Lending Practices: Treatment of Businesses in Distress*. Available at: http://www.tomlinsonreport. com/docs/tomlinsonReport.pdf (accessed December 2013).

Treanor, J. (2013) 'Vince Cable backs independence of Tomlinson report on RBS'. *Guardian*, 5 December 2013.

uSwitch (2013) 'Not a single UK city is "super-fast" for broadband yet'. Available at: http://www.uswitch.com/media-centre/2013/10/not-a-single-uk-city-is-super-fast-for-broadband-yet/ (accessed January 2014).

Vickers, J. and Yarrow, G. (1988) *Privatisation. An Economic Analysis*. Cambridge, MA: MIT Press.

Virgin (2013) *Annual Report and Accounts 2013*.

Vivid Economics (2011) *The Green Investment Bank: Policy and Finance Context. Report Prepared for the Department of Business Innovation and Skills*. Available at: https://www.gov.uk/govern ment/uploads/system/uploads/attachment_data/file/31757/12-553-green-investment-bank-policy-and-finance-context.pdf (accessed December 2013).

Wallerstein, I. (1991) 'Braudel on capitalism, or everything upside down'. *Journal of Modern History*, 63: 356–61.

Wallop, H. (2013) 'Supermarkets: British shoppers' fatal attraction'. *Telegraph*, 4 March 2013.

Wheatley, J.R. (1986) 'Competition, privatisation and change at British Telecom'. *Technovation*, 5: 115–24.

Which? (2012) 'Supermarket special offers exposed'. *Which?*, June 2012: 22-5. Available at: http://www.which.co.uk/documents/pdf/ p22-25_supermarketspecials-286314.pdf (accessed January 2014).

Which? (2013) 'Cost of PPI scandal now more than double the cost of the Olympics'. Press Release, 1 August 2013. Available at: https:// press.which.co.uk/whichstatements/cost-of-ppi-scandal-now-more-than-double-the-cost-of-the-olympics/ (accessed December 2013).

Wik Consult (2013) 'Estimating the cost of GEA: confidential study for TalkTalk'. Available at: http://br0kent3l3ph0n3.files. wordpress.com/2013/05/wik-report-on-gea-costing.pdf (accessed January 2014).

Willcox, W. (2012) 'Updated history of Ewhurst Broadband'. Available at: http://www.ewhurst-broadband.org.uk/?p=1893 (accessed December 2013).

Willcox, W. and Coope, D. (2013) 'Superfast broadband performance in Ewhurst, Surrey'. Available at: http://www.texp.co.uk/downloads/Broadband%20Performance%20Ewhurst%20-%20 Issue%202.pdf (accessed December 2013).

Willets, D. (2013) *Eight Great Technologies*. London: Policy Exchange.

Williams, C. (2013) 'George Osborne broadband growth plan abandoned over state aid complaints'. *Daily Telegraph*, 26 June 2013.

Williams, E.E. (1896) *Made in Germany*. London: Heinemann.

Williams, K., Williams, J., Haslam, C. and Thomas, D. (1981) *Why are the British Bad at Manufacturing?* London: Routledge.

Wood, Z. (2012) 'Tesco shake-up after £5bn battering'. *The Guardian*, 12 January 2012.

WRAP (2011) *The Water and Carbon Footprint of Household Food and Drink Waste in the UK*. Available at: http://www.wrap.org.uk/sites/files/wrap/Water%20and%20Carbon%20Footprint%20 report%20Final%2C%20Nov%202011.pdf (accessed December 2013).

YouGov (2013) 'Nationalise energy and rail companies, British public say'. Available at: http://yougov.co.uk/news/2013/11/04/nationalise-energy-and-rail-companies-say-public/ (accessed January 2014).